JUNE   EVENING

A Play in Two Acts

by

Bill Naughton

FOR AMATEUR PRODUCTION ENQUIRIES

UNITED KINGDOM AND WORLD
EXCLUDING NORTH AMERICA

plays@samuelfrench.co.uk

020 7255 4302/01

Each title is subject to availability from Samuel French, depending upon country of performance.

LIST OF CHARACTERS

SARAH KIPPAX

BEATTY KIPPAX   (her daughter-in-law)

ALBERT KIPPAX   (her son)

JACK HARWOOD

POLLY HARWOOD

FANNY BRIGHOUSE   (Polly's Mother)

LIZ SEDWIN

HARRY SEDWIN

MISS PRATT   (Midwife)

OLIVE WHITTLE

The action of the play takes place in and
around a street in Bolton on the evening
of June 1st, 1921

*   *   *

ACT ONE

Scene One	=	Kippax Front Kitchen
Scene Two	=	Corner Shop
Scene Three	=	Street

ACT TWO

Scene One	=	Kippax Front Kitchen
Scene Two	=	Corner Shop
Scene Three	=	Harwood's Backyard
Scene Four	=	Harwood's Front Kitchen
Scene Five	=	Harwood's Front Kitchen

ACT ONE   Scene One

House lights go down and we hear the singing
of children in the street, with a street song
of the 1920's (The Wind or the Lusitania).
Curtain rises on the front kitchen of a cottage
in a Lancashire industrial street. It is a
summer evening in 1921. Slowly sneak away
the singing. The scene is realised with two or
three simple but evocative items such as a
rocking chair, fender, and cradle. The feeling
evoked must be warm and homely and not drab
in any way. There are two entrances, one
leading to the back kitchen and the other opening
on to the strip of street outside. SARAH
KIPPAX, seated on the rocking chair with the
fender in front of her, is down front facing the
audience. She is a woman in her sixties,
wearing blouse and skirt, and talks in a flat
and forthright manner, seemingly unemotional,
without a trace of self-pity, and the odd touch
of humour, often sly, is never wholly absent.
BEATTY KIPPAX is humming a lullaby as she
rocks the cradle. She has the air of a rather
confident young mother, not unkind, but
removed from the world of the older woman.
After a lengthy pause we see that SARAH has
some crafty thought on her mind.

SARAH   (hesitant: air of innocence) I say, Beatty, when are we
                 going to have our tea?

                 BEATTY can never be sure when
                 SARAH is coming it.

BEATTY   Tea ... you've had your tea.

SARAH   I have ... well, that's news to me.

BEATTY   Don't you remember ... just before five o'clock.

SARAH   You mean that lettuce butty! ... were that supposed to
                 be our tea!

BEATTY   And you'd an Ormskirk gingerbread as well ... and a second
                 mug of tea. We're not living in Buckingham Palace, yu'know
                 two teas in one day. I can't think what I'll give your Albert
                 when he gets home.

SARAH	I wouldn't have golloped it down so fast if I'd known. Course there's not much to get your teeth into in a lettuce butty. I wouldn't say no to a bite of something that's looked over a fence for a change.
BEATTY	That's what?
SARAH	A slice of roast beef, or a nice bit of steak or even a lamb chop.
BEATTY	We might get some neck of mutton on Friday for a broth. That's if your Albert gets any strike pay this week.

Knocking heard off.

JACK HARWOOD	(off) Hello there! Anybody in?

JACK pops his head round door.

SARAH	(cheerfully) Come in, Jack, and let's have a look at you.

JACK HARWOOD enters from the Back Kitchen. He is in his twenties, a miner, open and natural.

JACK	Howgo, Mrs Kippax.
SARAH	Nice to see you, love.
BEATTY	Hello, Jack.
JACK	Hello, Beatty. I'm not disturbing your tea, am I?
SARAH	What tea ... oh, no - he's not disturbing our tea, is he, Beatty!
BEATTY	No - we've had it.
SARAH	Oh, aye - I forgot - we're nearly ready for supper.
JACK	(looks round) Is your Albert in?
BEATTY	No, he's gone to th'allotment, gettin' maggots for his fishing. Not that he ever brings any fish home.
SARAH	Ee, I wouldn't eat fish out of the canal, the folk as have drowned 'emselves in there this last twelve month.

JACK	I only wanted to know had he finished with white wash brush. Polly wants it to whitewash the petty.
BEATTY	How's she feeling?
JACK	Champion ... now she's over all that heartburn.
BEATTY	She'll not have long to go will Polly.
JACK	Miss Pratt reckons another three weeks.
SARAH	Hair.
JACK	What?
SARAH	I said hair.
JACK	That's what I thought you said.
SARAH	The child's hair causes heartburn. You can expect it to have a lot of hair when it's born. And I'd say it was a boy the way she's carrying it out front.
BEATTY	Old wives' tales. I'll get you that brush, Jack.

BEATTY exits into Back Kitchen.

SARAH	(nods after BEATTY) She's had one of her own so she knows it all.
JACK	Polly's had a right attack of cleaning - she's swilled the yard - and just done the upstairs -
SARAH	It sounds to me that Polly could be nearer her time than she thinks.
JACK	Oh,no - Miss Pratt reckons ...
SARAH	(cuts in) Aye, but the child has never heard of Miss Pratt, and when the time comes for it to come it'll come.

During this SARAH has furtively taken
two pennies out of her purse.

Here y'are, Jack - get yourself a packet of Woodbines.

SARAH hands the pennies to JACK.

JACK	Nay, I couldn't.

SARAH thrusts the coppers into
JACK's hand and puts a finger
to her lips.

SARAH   It's nowt to what your mother did for my lads.

JACK   Aye, well, it was like they were her own. She never
rightly got over it.   Ee, but ta - I could do with a smoke.

SARAH   It's not only that Polly'll be wanting everything spick and
span - but she'll be easing herself into the bargain. And I
expect your nerves are getting a bit on edge, love.

JACK   They are now.   It wasn't so bad the early months - and
I was working, too, so it took my mind off things - but now
the time's drawing closer, and I'm beside her day and night
it all seems such a mystery I get frightened.

SARAH   It is a mystery, love.

JACK   And I don't seem to have the confidence a father should
have.

SARAH   It's being on strike, lad - idleness seems to sap a man's
spirit - but it'll come, once you hold him in your arms.
It's a kind of faith or something - and it's there if you need
it enough.

JACK   Well, I hope it's not denied me.

BEATTY enters with brush.

BEATTY   Here's your brush, Jack.

JACK   Ta, Beatty.   'To SARAH) Then I've got this feeling Polly
would sooner not have me round the place.

BEATTY   Well, a chap out on strike is neither use nor ornament.

SARAH   Nay, it's not that Jack - it's that she's getting drawn closer
to the infant inside her, see. But once he's born she'll be
her old self again.

JACK   I hope so. Course she's not demonstrative at the best of
time, isn't Polly. She misses her mother but won't admit
it.

BEATTY   You'd have thought they'd have patched up that quarrel by
this.

JACK   They're each waiting for t'other to make the first move. Ee, but she misses their cup of tea together - and the little chats they always had.

SARAH   That reminds me - Beatty, we haven't offered Jack a cup of tea, have we?

                       SARAH contrives not to see BEATTY's look.

BEATTY   Jack, would you - ?

JACK   I wouldn't say no if I were asked.

SARAH   She needs somebody to give her a good talking to.

                       JACK swells up with misplaced confidence. BEATTY reluctantly sets about making tea.

JACK   I think that's exactly what I'll do - knock a bit of sense into her.

                       POLLY HARWOOD's voice is heard off, loud and demanding.

POLLY   (yells, off) Ja'ack! Ja'ack! ... Where've you got to!

JACK   (jumps) Eee, that's her now - I'd best be off ... (Calls) All right, Polly ... coming!

                       POLLY HARWOOD enters. She is young and pregnant.

POLLY   It's only me. (To JACK) Hey, you, how much longer are you going to be with that whitewash brush!

JACK   I were just coming, Polly.

POLLY   Vamoose!

                       JACK grabs brush and with comic haste makes towards door.

SARAH   (calls after him) Hy, Jack ... you haven't heard what won t'Derby, have you?

JACK   Eh? What? The Derby? Oh, they said something about favourite.

SARAH   Were that Humorist?

JACK	(departing) No - I think it were Craig an Eran.
SARAH	Blast it ...
JACK	I'll mix whitewash for you, Polly.

JACK exits.

POLLY	Flamin' useless lot are men!
BEATTY	How are you keeping, Polly?
POLLY	Champion - if it weren't for yon fellow! I'd best go and keep an eye on him or he'll be making a mess of it. So long now.

POLLY exits.

BEATTY	I won't need to bother with that tea now. (To SARAH) Why were you asking about Derby? Have you been backing horses!

Start to sneak in the sound of children
singing street song, off:

THE WIND BLOWS HIGH
(The Girl of the Golden City)

The wind, the wind, the wind blows high,
Rain comes scattering from the sky,
Winnie Whittle says she'll die,
For the want of the Golden City.

She is handsome,
She is pretty,
She is the flower of the Golden City,
She has a lover, one, two, three,
Pray now tell me who he'll be.

SARAH	Eh? Oh ... aye - I had my yearly flutter on the Derby. I put my last bob on Steve. I dreamt last night he won on Humorist - I saw 'em going first past post. But it's getting as you can't even trust your dreams these days. You know what I thought - I thought, if he's won, I'll treat us all to some roast pork and stuffin' for tea!
BEATTY	You know what thought did - followed a muck cart an' thought it were a wedding. Besides, you've had your tea. Just think what we could have bought with that shilling!

                    The CHILDREN's voices off reach a
crescendo as they end their song and
chant:
"Me not! Me not! Me not!"

                    The noise wakens the BABY and it
starts to cry. BEATTY turns and
gives a hurried shake to the cradle
and hushes the child, then runs to the
door.

BEATTY   (yells) Hey - you lot! Clear off with your din! Go on!
Sling your hook! I won't tell you again - I'll come and clatter
your earholes for you!

                    CHILDREN off: muttering and rude
noises, as they move away. Song
starts up again, receding.

Cheeky little hussies.

                    BEATTY moves back to cradle.

SARAH   Have you driven childer away from front door!

BEATTY   Aye - I have - what about it.

SARAH   Children have been playing outside that door for the past
fifty years as I know of.

BEATTY   Then it's time they went and played somewhere else.

SARAH   I wish you hadn't sent 'em away, Beatty. They're company
to me, those children's voices. I remember my own boys
playing their games outside there, our Frank and Sammy,
and young Jimmy with his trolley. Yu'know there are times
when I rest back in this chair and I feel I can still hear
them.

                    FADE UP distant singing of children.
SARAH rests back in her chair.
BEATTY preserves an air of resigned
silence and busies herself with folding
baby clothes. Something suddenly takes
SARAH's attention and she rises to her
feet and stares in front of her at the
mantelpiece.

SARAH   Hy - what have you been up to?

BEATTY   What's wrong now?

SARAH   Where's my lads' picture gone?

BEATTY   Which one?

SARAH   The picture of my three sons - you know which one - the photo they had taken in their uniforms when they all three came home on furlough, Christmas 1915. It were standing there on t'mantelpiece where it always stands ...

BEATTY   I put it over there. On t'dresser. I thought our Wellington's photo looked nice there.

> BEATTY comes up and looks with some pride at picture.

SARAH   Well, would you take it away again, and let me have my sons' picture back, please.

> BEATTY picks up the picture, and goes and places it on the dresser, then takes up another picture, comes across and hands it to SARAH. SARAH wipes it with her pinafore and puts it up on the mantelpiece.

You can feel and hold your child any time you want, but I'll never see a sight of my three lads again. Their King and bloody country claimed 'em, to make this a land fit for heroes to live in! Aye, and same as they say, you need to be a flamin' hero to live in it.

> ALBERT KIPPAX enters. He is a young man, wearing the clogs, cap and scarf and other gear of the miner who is not working. His manner is quiet and gentle; the smile leaves his face as he quickly senses the tension in the home.

SARAH   (covering up) Are you back, son?

ALBERT   Yes, mam.

BEATTY   Did you get your maggots?

ALBERT   Eh ... no, I did a bit of digging instead. An' I fetched a few flowers home.

> ALBERT takes a bunch of nice flowers
> which he has had hidden under his jacket
> and puts them down.

ALBERT   It's lovely outside. Folk are sitting out on their chairs
up an' down the street.

> Neither BEATTY nor SARAH thank
> ALBERT for the flowers, and there
> is a full moment of unspoken feeling
> between the trio, which ALBERT breaks.

Think I'll go an' wash me, an' take mi clogs off.

> ALBERT exits to the back kitchen.

SARAH   ... Is everything all right between you two?

BEATTY   (quick defence) Oh, yes. Nothing wrong between us. Why?

SARAH   (leaves the matter) I'm sorry, Beatty love ... about my
little outburst.

BEATTY   (detached) It's all right. I understand.

SARAH   (flat) I'm afraid you don't, love. You've got to be old
yourself to understand old age. What I wouldn't give just
to feel I were wanted in some way - to know that somebody
needed me. Instead I feel I'm just wasting good bread.

BEATTY   We'st not have to give you so much then. Oh, and that
reminds me - we've none left for his tea. I'd best go to
the corner shop.

> BEATTY picks up a cardigan (hug-
> me-tight, as they were called).
> SARAH turns to the flowers, taking
> them out one by one.

SARAH   Yu'know what - they said I'd never rear him.

BEATTY   Rear who?

> BEATTY seldom listens very
> attentively to SARAH.

SARAH   (still arranging flowers) Our Albert.   He wasn't much
              bigger than my fist he wasn't, when he were born. And
              he'd bronchitis very bad. I wore out many a set of clog
              irons carrying him around the neighbourhood under mi
              shawl, looking for these gangs of corporation workmen
              tarring the roads.

BEATTY   (interested) Whatever for?

SARAH   I'd get the watchman to hoist up the lid of one of the boiling
              tar tanks, so that the poor lad could get just a whiff of the
              fumes. It was the only thing that would ease his chest. Made
              him cough, see, and bring it all up. Used to beat all your
              Friars' Balsam.
                         BEATTY seems quite touched by
                         the story and is drawn to confide
                         something in SARAH.

BEATTY   To be honest, he has been a bit off, like, of late ... you
              know what I mean ... he's not been himself in more ways
              than one, if you follow me.

                         This is a very deep exchange indeed
                         for BEATTY to make and SARAH has
                         to think about it.

SARAH   It's the strike, I expect, worrying the poor lad. It seems
              to have that effect on the home life. His Dad were the same
              now I come to think of it.   Weren't much use for anything
              when he were on strike. I expect he'll make up for it when
              he gets back to his work. I know his Dad always did.

                         ALBERT, in stockinged feet, appears
                         at door to Back Kitchen, unseen by
                         SARAH and BEATTY. He has a towel
                         in his hand, and is drying his face.
                         He stands silent.

              Ee, but same as I were saying, I'll never forget one time
              I was holding our little Albert up over the tank of bubbling
              tar, and this watchman is looking at his little purple
              spluttering face, and he turns to me an' he says ... If I
              were you, Missis, know what I'd do - drop the little sod
              in ...

                         A faint smile comes to ALBERT's face,
                         as we FADE OUT.

During the scene change, we fade
up the sound of the children singing
street songs (off).

* * *

ACT ONE   Scene Two

The Corner Shop.

We get an impression of an old-fashioned
mixed groceries shop. There is a counter,
with cash drawer, possibly a chair, or a
sack of flour which can be used as a seat.
There is a big strap book on the counter,
dirty and dog-eared.
LIZ SEDWIN, a generous-natured woman
is serving BEATTY.

BEATTY   ... Oh, and could I have two ounces of best butter, please.

LIZ   Course you could -

BEATTY   For old Sarah, see - I'll give her a surprise with her toast
              in the morning.

LIZ   How is Sarah - I hardly seem to have seen her of late.

BEATTY   She stands at back door mostly - feeding the birds. She
              doesn't like to come out the front. Seems to have lost
              pride in herself.

LIZ   Aye, what she had pride in has been taken away from her.

BEATTY   You know, they'll eat off her hand.

LIZ   Well, it's a comfort at the end of your days to know that
              some living creature needs you, even if it's only a sparrow
              in the street.

                        Enter MISS PRATT during this.

MISS PRATT   Are not sparrows sold for two a farthing in the market
              place, yet one shall not fall from a tree without thy
              Father - A bottle of castor oil, please.

LIZ   Yes, Miss Pratt.

                        LIZ turns to get bottle.
                        Enter HARRY SEDWIN, yawning. He
                        is in his forties - bluff, crafty, genial.
                        He is wearing an open-necked khaki
                        shirt, braces, trousers and slippers.

LIZ   (to HARRY) I thought you were never going to wake up!
              He'd win a prize for sleeping!

HARRY   I think I'd a touch of the old malaria come back.

LIZ   You mean all the flamin' ale you supped at dinner-time -
               that's what gave you the shivers!

HARRY   I only sup it to keep up my betting custom!

MISS PRATT   (to BEATTY) Were you talking of your mother-in-law,
               Sarah Kippax?

BEATTY   Yes, why?

MISS PRATT   That woman used to be a pillar of this neighbourhood. She
               was on hand at every birth in this street - in spite of having
               four lads of her own to take care of. (Takes castor oil)
               Thank you.

HARRY   You keeping busy, Miss Pratt?

MISS PRATT   Busy! I'm just rushing over to Bessemer Street with this -
               a woman in labour and hadn't taken her castor oil - and do
               you know why? - she hadn't a penny in the house to buy it.
               (Puts sixpence on counter)

LIZ   They keep you in demand. (Gives change)

HARRY   Aye, there's no poverty between the sheets. Eh, Beatty?
               Ee, but I wish I were in demand.

LIZ   Who'd demand you!

HARRY   You get many a good tune played on an old fiddle - what do
               you say, Miss Pratt?

MISS PRATT   I've heard it said - but they're tunes I'd prefer not to hear.
               Goodbye.

                         MISS PRATT exits.

HARRY   Toodlepip.

                    LIZ marks BEATTY's credit book.

               Have you heard what's won the Derby, Beatty?

BEATTY   I've heard what's not won it - Humorist.

HARRY   (brightens up) Is that so?

BEATTY   Yes, Sarah lost a bob on it.

HARRY   Bloody good ... somehow I knew it! I might take you out
            tonight, Liz, after we've closed up.

                    The sudden good mood prompts HARRY
                    to put a sly arm round LIZ. LIZ is
                    always suspicious of HARRY in this mood
                    and pushes him away.

LIZ   What the hell's come over you! (To BEATTY) Talking of
            Sarah, just hang on a tick, Beatty, I think I've something
            for her.

                    LIZ exits to the shop kitchen. HARRY is
                    still delighted with the news and moves
                    round the counter.

HARRY   I said Steve Donoghue wouldn't win... I knew it in my
            bones ... How's married life going, Beatty?

BEATTY   All right, thank you!

HARRY   Ee, but you must be in right good buckle.

                    HARRY puts his arm round BEATTY.

BEATTY   Keep your maulers to yourself, will you!

                    LIZ enters, carrying large, steaming
                    plate, covered with paper, and spots
                    HARRY.

BEATTY   Ooh, what's that - that smells good.

HARRY   Roast heart.

LIZ   Yes, I did it this afternoon, with sage and onion stuffing.

                    LIZ puts the plate on the counter and
                    removes paper, revealing a roast ox
                    heart.

            Now, how much would you like - a quarter pound, a half -
            or what ... ?

                    BEATTY stares down at it longingly
                    then changes her mind.

BEATTY	Ee, no I daren't!
LIZ	Why not?
BEATTY	I've overshot my credit mark as it is - I don't know when I'll get straight -
LIZ	Don't worry - it won't always be dark at seven -

        LIZ has cut a slice and holds it at
        the end of the knife for BEATTY.

Here, just sample it, love.

        HARRY watches bemused. BEATTY
        looks hungrily at meat but shakes
        her head.

BEATTY	No! No! I mustn't!

        BEATTY grabs her groceries and
        makes off.

        HARRY takes piece of meat and eats
        it.

LIZ	(to BEATTY) Hy! ... I say ...

        BEATTY stops and looks.

BEATTY	Yes?
LIZ	Tak' Sarah a quarter from me.
BEATTY	No - I daren't go into debt any more.

        LIZ begins to cut into roast heart.

LIZ	Give over - it's on the house. A treat.
BEATTY	Ee, she'd never forgive me ... accepting anything. She's proud is Sarah ... very proud ... Ta, just the same.

        BEATTY exits.

LIZ	Well, bless me - half the street starvin' and I can't give it away ...

LIZ enters credit in strapbook.

HARRY   You been lettin' Kippax's have more tick?

LIZ   What else would I do when folk are in need?

HARRY   The whole bloody town's in need. You've got to draw a
               line somewhere.

LIZ   They've never missed paying from that house.

HARRY   Well, let's hope they go on paying.

LIZ   I'm not only in business - I've got my good name to
               keep up, haven't I?

HARRY   There's no profit in that.

LIZ   Profit! - Is that all you think about?

HARRY   What else is there to think about in a shop?

LIZ   My mother and her mother before her ran this shop -
               they're gone now, God rest 'em, but they left a good
               name behind in this street and I'm determined it'll stay
               that way. Of course, you wouldn't know anything about
               that -
                              LIZ takes roast heart to kitchen.

HARRY   (huffed) Wouldn't I? Don't you be too sure - I've had
               my testing time - it was a long way from this street -
               it was in the bloody desert - but I think I came through.
               Aye, and with a good name.

                              JACK HARWOOD enters, looking
                              mithered, with a small shopping
                              basket and an envelope on which
                              notes are written.

               Now, Jack, what can I do for you?

JACK   (reads) Could I have a Monkey Brand, a Scrubbing brush,
               and a bar of blue carbolic soap, an' a packet of Hudson's
               soap powder... oh, and rubbing stones.

                              LIZ re-enters during this.

LIZ   Somebody's having a cleaning fit - and of a Wednesday!

JACK   It's Polly. Her's whitewashing, and her wants closet floor scrubbing an' everything. She's on the go every second.

HARRY   Her must be gettin' near her droppin' time, must Polly -

LIZ   Don't you come out with that vulgar talk, Harry Sedwin! Say confinement - you're talking about a lady.

JACK   Ee, but I'll be right glad when this coal strike's over -

HARRY   So will we, Mate. Harken that till - three ha'pence in it. Hasta heard what's won t' Derby?

JACK   I heard summat about favourite.

HARRY   (eagerly) Aye, Craig an Eran. Bloody good, I knew Steve couldn't win.

LIZ   Why're you so pleased about him not winning - what difference does it make to you - you're only the bookies' runner.

HARRY   (changes subject) No, Jack, you miners are the same as other working folk - you've been living in a Utopia for years with the war on, and now that it's over, you can't get it into your heads you're not essential any more.

JACK   I've got it now though.

LIZ   Don't be silly, love, you're more essential than ever now. You're going to become a father.

HARRY   They think that's the only reason for a man's existence. But I'll give you miners credit for one thing - you've stuck together.

JACK   Well, down the pit your mate's trouble is your trouble.

HARRY   But what bloody fools you were to imagine at a time like this you could beat the mine owners. I'll bet none of them is buying rubbing stones on the strap. You certainly picked a nice time to become a daddy.

JACK   I didn't pick it, it picked me. A packet of Woodbines. An' I'll pay cash down for 'em - there's my twopence.

HARRY   Ta. That'll come in very handy. (Loudly drops two pennies in empty till.

JACK takes cigarette from packet
and lights it. Then he sees HARRY
watching him, waiting, and offers
the packet to him.

JACK   Will you have one?

HARRY   Ta. (Takes cigarette)

LIZ   You're taking the poor chap's cigarettes now.

HARRY   There's nothing more frustrating when you have nowt,
                than folk refusing what bit you have.

JACK   Could I have two rubbing stones - a donkey an' a yellow.

LIZ   She has got a bout of the cleaners on her.

JACK   She's set on doing the doorstep an' the windowsill tonight.

LIZ   It's natural she should want everything spick and span
                before the happy event.

HARRY   Yon bitch of ours, Bess, were just the same every time
                she were going to have pups. Fussing about her kennel
                and begging for clean newspapers. I suppose it's just the
                same with a pregnant woman. You could say she was
                preparing for pupping.

                        LIZ gives HARRY a hard dig because
                        POLLY HARWOOD enters during this.
                        POLLY overheards HARRY, gives him
                        a look, but refrains at that moment
                        from saying anything. She is carrying
                        a saucer.

LIZ   (quickly) Hello, Polly, love!

HARRY   (loudly) Jack, here's your missis. Howgo, Polly?

JACK   (anxiously) Ee, hello! Are you all right, Polly?
                Nothing wrong is there?

POLLY   Course I'm all right. Where've you been, you great big
                slowcoach? You know I'm in a hurry. (Grabs packet of
                soap powder) Where's my scrubbing brush and carbolic?

JACK   They're here, love, they're here.

POLLY
I see you got yourself a smoke. (To LIZ) I pity you, Liz. I never realized what it was to have a chap under your feet for twenty-four hours a day.

HARRY
You'll miss him when he goes back to work - especially at nights.

LIZ gives HARRY a dig.

I mean for keeping her feet warm - what's up with you?

POLLY
(to HARRY) Here, what were you saying just now about a pregnant woman and a bitch having pups?

HARRY
It's one and the same instinct, isn't it - giving birth - in a bitch and a woman, eh, Jack?

JACK
I don't know anything about dogs.

HARRY
It's even the same with a camel in the desert. I've known them go off and make themselves a little spotless hide-away when their time's come.

LIZ
(changing subject) What's the saucer for, love? Did you want something?

POLLY
Aye. Two penn'orth of mustard pickles, please.

JACK
Who do you want pickles for?

POLLY
For me - who do you think?

LIZ
Ee, I don't think I'd have any mustard pickles if I were you, Polly.

POLLY
Sorry, Liz, I've got to have them. I'll go mad if I don't. I were just swilling the backyard down and cleaning the stuff when suddenly I got this over-powering longing for a nice juicy mustard pickle -

HARRY
A little of what you fancy -

HARRY gets pickle jar.

POLLY
Ee, I can't wait a second longer - give us one of them pickles.

HARRY holds out a large wooden spoonful.

HARRY   Tak' your pick.

JACK   But Polly -

POLLY   Shut your gob. I'll have a gherkin - no I won't, I'll have
           an onion - ta.

                         The trio gaze with different expressions
                         at POLLY as she takes the mustard
                         pickle, pops it in her mouth and gives
                         a sharp crunch, a chew, and swallows
                         it.

POLLY   By gum, that tasted good. I feel better already.

                         Enter FANNY BRIGHOUSE during
                         this. She is POLLY's mother, a
                         widow, about 40, neat, warm, a
                         woman of principle. She is unseen
                         by POLLY. JACK and LIZ react.

LIZ   (quietly) Polly, your mother!

HARRY   (breezily) Hello there, Fanny!

                         POLLY turns and sees FANNY.
                         Her manner changes.

POLLY   (to LIZ) Excuse me, I've got to be off.

HARRY   Aren't you waiting for your mustard pickles!

POLLY   Jack can bring 'em.

                         As POLLY turns to go she drops
                         the packet of soap powder. FANNY
                         stoops down and picks it up. There
                         is a moment's silence as FANNY and
                         POLLY face each other. Then POLLY
                         takes the packet.

           (icy politeness) Thank you.

                         POLLY exits.

FANNY   What do you think of that, Liz - my own daughter ...!

JACK   I'm sorry, Ma, but you know what she's like.

FANNY	Went off without a word! My own flesh and blood!
LIZ	She didn't mean anything. You could see she was upset.
FANNY	What about me? Her mother who brought her into the world!
HARRY	Fanny, the way things are going on, you'll soon be a grandma.
FANNY	I don't want to hear anything further about it! A quarter of tea, please, and a Dolly blue.
LIZ	(getting things) Now, don't say that, Fanny, because you know it's not true.
FANNY	Did you see how she went off and never spoke a word to her own mother?
HARRY	Why didn't you speak to her?
FANNY	Eh? Who? Me? Why should I speak? It wasn't my place.
HARRY	What's it all about? What upset you at the start?
FANNY	When a neighbour can come into my home and tell me my daughter's expecting a baby and me knowing nothing about it, then I think I've every right to feel upset.
JACK	She were only guessing. I tell you Polly never told anybody! I didn't even know myself she were like that.
FANNY	There's no need for you to know. You're only the husband. A mother is different. The first person a wife should go and tell is her own mother. I told mine, didn't you, Liz?
LIZ	No - she told me. There's your Dolly blue.
HARRY	Here's your pickles, Jack.
FANNY	Who's them pickles for?
HARRY	For your Polly.
JACK	She had a sudden fancy for 'em.
FANNY	For mustard pickles! Don't tell me that!
LIZ	She were eating one when you came in. Said she couldn't wait.

FANNY   Oh, poor girl!

LIZ   Why, what's up, Fanny?

FANNY   When I were carrying her I couldn't look a pickle in the eye for months on end, and suddenly one dinner-time as I were scrubbing the back steps I got this longing for a mustard pickle.

JACK   What about it?

FANNY   An hour later our Polly were well on the way.

HARRY   Give over, Fanny, look at the poor father - he's gone white! Fancy a sup of water, Jack?

FANNY   (looks at plateful of pickles in JACK's hand. To HARRY) Hy, you call them pickles! They're all flamin' cauliflower and cabbage - give the lass some cucumber, gherkins and onions.

HARRY   How many damn gherkins and onions do you think you get for tuppence? You're not in India.

FANNY   Those pickles are for a pregnant woman.

LIZ   Of course they are! Get out of the way -

HARRY   If I made exceptions for every pregnant woman in this street, we'd be bloody bankrupt. And we're damn near that as it is.

                LIZ puts big spoonful of pickles on
                plate.

LIZ   How's that, Fanny?

FANNY   That's more like it.

HARRY   That's where all the profits go.

JACK   Ta, Mrs Sedwin - I'll be off.

FANNY   I'd like a word with you, Jack. (To LIZ) How much do I owe you, Liz?

LIZ   Sevenpence.

FANNY   I think I've got right change. (Hands coins out of purse) Here y'are, Liz.

HARRY   We're doing well ...

            PAPERMAN's bell is heard, off.

PAPERMAN   (off) Evening News - six o'clock edition ... all the news and winners ...

HARRY   Paperchap! - I'll get paper.

FANNY   I'll be off, Liz.

LIZ   Ta ra,. Fanny.

            HARRY has taken his handkerchief out of his trouser pocket, and some curled-up slips of paper drop out. HARRY is too interested in getting the Evening News to notice, and as he hurries out he also gives a sexy pat to FANNY on her bottom.

HARRY   Ooh, you're in grand fettle, Fanny! ...

            HARRY exits with a loud whistle after the paperchap. FANNY looks after him in contempt and then goes to JACK who is waiting for her outside the shop.

            FADE DOWN on shop. interior where LIZ can faintly be seen to be quietly tidying things. FADE UP on JACK and FANNY in street.

JACK   What is it, Ma ?

FANNY   Jack, love - should our Polly start off - you know what I mean - you'll come and let me know straight away, won't you - promise -

JACK   I promise.

FANNY   Or if she so much as asks for me - you won't hesitate, you'll come running at once.

JACK   I will. But couldn't you just come over with me now - she'd give anything to have you near.

FANNY   Nay, Jack, I mustn't - because our Polly would never forgive herself if she thought she'd made her mother make the first move. I love the girl too much to cause her any distress. God bless.

> FANNY exits, very moved but trying to hide it. JACK exits, hurrying.
>
> FADE UP shop interior.
>
> LIZ has been seen to pick up the papers HARRY dropped and has got them unrolled and is reading them on the counter.

LIZ   (reads) Humorist, threepence each way. Humorist, sixpenc win. Humorist, shilling win ... Humorist ... Humorist ...

> Re-enter HARRY carrying newspaper, and with air of anticipatory pleasure. LIZ swiftly puts betting slips out of sight into her pinafore pocket.

HARRY   Where's mi specs, Liz?

LIZ   Here - you'll be needing 'em!

> LIZ hands HARRY small case and watches him closely as HARRY takes out wire spectacles and with a lordly air, puts them on and opens the paper.

HARRY   (reads) Miners' leaders won't give in. They'll hatta bloody give in. Now, where's the racing ... here we are ... Humorist ... Humorist wins Derby ... get off, must be a bloody misprint ... Humorist - Steve Donoghue, six to one .. it can't be!

LIZ   What's up? You look as though you've seen a ghost.

HARRY   Read that for me, will you, Liz. There - the Derby ...

LIZ   (reads) Humorist, one, Craig an Eran -

HARRY   But they said Humorist had lost - and it's bloody won!

LIZ   What about it -

HARRY   That bloody Steve Donoghue -you can't trust the bloody Irish. Everybody's followed him. There'll be pounds to pay out.

LIZ   What're you worrying about - it's the bookies will have to
             pay out, not you ... you're only the runner!

HARRY   Who'd have bloody thought it - Humorist!

                     HARRY takes handkerchief out and
                     wipes his brow. LIZ watches him
                     closely and HARRY knows he's being
                     watched.

LIZ   Have you been up to your tricks again?

HARRY   What tricks? Eh! - I've been up to no tricks.

LIZ   Salting the betting slips - taking out the bets you thought
             would lose. Making yourself a few bob on the sly ...

HARRY   Certainly not. What do you think I am!

LIZ   Then what about these ... eh?

                     LIZ takes slips from apron pocket.

             (reads) Humorist, threepence each way, Humorist,
             shilling win, Humorist ...

HARRY   Where'd you get them?

LIZ   They dropped out of your bloody pocket ...

                     HARRY is cornered for one moment
                     and then comes across with his excuse.

HARRY   Oh, good Christ - I musta stuffed 'em in the wrong pocket
             by mistake ...

LIZ   You bloody liar ... you've been swindling - and you've
             come unstuck. I curse the day I ever let you bring a
             betting slip into my shop.

HARRY   Liz, I can swear on my ...

                     Enter OLIVE WHITTLE. HARRY
                     shuts up as soon as he spots her.

OLIVE   Swear what?

HARRY   Nothing ...

LIZ   (covering up) Hello, Olive. What would you like?

OLIVE   I've come to collect my winnings.

HARRY   What winnings?

OLIVE   On the Derby - what d'you think? Has he not been to the bookies yet?

LIZ   He'll be going. Was there anything else?

OLIVE   I fancy summat good ...

LIZ   I've got the very thing.

         LIZ exits to kitchen. OLIVE puts
         an eye on HARRY and waves a sheet
         of paper.

OLIVE   I've lots of bets here to draw on Humorist.

HARRY   You don't say!

OLIVE   So I want time to check all the amounts to see they're right.

HARRY   They're always right when I pay out.

         Re-enter LIZ carrying roast heart
         with paper over.

OLIVE   The sooner you get started the better. D'you know who gave me the Humorist tip - Sarah Kippax. She dreamt last night she saw him go past the post.

HARRY   (aside) Aye, an' I wish he'd fell off an' broke his bloody neck.

         LIZ removes paper with a flourish.

LIZ   Now what about that, Olive? Lovely ox heart.

         OLIVE gives it a long dubious look.
         LIZ picks up carving knife.

OLIVE   I fancied summat a bit tastier than heart - being as I've backed the Derby winner.

LIZ   There's sage and onion stuffing to go with it.

OLIVE   I'm sure it's very nice. But not exactly for celebrating on ... you haven't roast pork, have you ...

LIZ   Not till Friday, love ... Friday's roast pork day.

OLIVE   Aye, so it is ...

                                  LIZ looks at knife in her hand and looks at HARRY and we get an idea of what she would like to do with the knife. So does HARRY.

What's he hanging about for!

LIZ   Don't worry, Olive - he'll be off any minute.

                                    OLIVE is not entirely satisfied and she sizes HARRY up.

OLIVE   You don't seem in any hurry.

HARRY   No, but I'll get there just the same.

OLIVE   Well, let's hope so. Because if you don't -

                                    OLIVE exits.

LIZ   What are you going to do about all the money owing on these bets!

                                    She takes slips from her pocket and waves them at HARRY.

HARRY   What can I do?

LIZ   Go an' tell the bookie what happened.

HARRY   I'd as soon gas meself.

LIZ   Then gas your bloody self! Before you show me up in front of my neighbours - you rotten ...

> LIZ makes a hysterical rush at
> HARRY and starts thumping him.

HARRY   (takes her wrists gently but firmly) Just a minute, lass -
you know I've had malaria ...

LIZ   You ... (Speechless)

> OLIVE re-enters. Stops short with
> surprise when she sees LIZ and HARRY.
> LIZ has her back to OLIVE, but HARRY
> sees her, takes hold of LIZ as though
> dancing·with her, and starts to hum a
> tune. LIZ cottons on. OLIVE is baffled.

OLIVE   I were going to say - don't forget. I'll be back later ...

HARRY   Any time you like ...

OLIVE   Ta ra, Liz.

LIZ   Ta ra.

> OLIVE, even more baffled, exits.
> LIZ disengages herself.

LIZ   What are we going to do! Don't you realise what you've
done! They'll be here any minute for their money. And
there's pounds to pay out. And these are poor folk who
only have a bet once a year - I can't let them down. I
must pay them. But where can I get money on a Wednesday
evening!

HARRY   Hy, Liz, you know "Ernie's - I buy anything" - the antique
and whatnot shop in Derby Street ... he's always open -
and he pays a good price for old gold, jewellery and the
like.

LIZ   Well, what use is that! ... (Realises) You mean sell my
things ... my gold chain locket, watch and rings! Why,
I'd never part with them. They were my mother's and her
mother's - they've been in the family for years.

HARRY   But what about your neighbours! I mean if they came -

LIZ   You put your jacket on, and go amongst all your boozing
mates and find some friend who'll lend you the money. I'll
see he gets paid back.

HARRY	There's not a man in civvy street I'd call a friend. I lost all my friends in Mesopotamia - fighting in the desert.
LIZ	You - you never had a friend!
HARRY	(unexpectedly hurt) Don't say a thing like that, Lizzie - please! Not for my sake but for theirs. You don't know what a pal is until you've been in the army. Why, I'd some of the dearest friends a man could wish to have. They'd lay down their life for me ... and by God, they did. May God rest 'em.

HARRY makes ready to go off.

LIZ	Where are you going?
HARRY	I'm going where I'll find some peace. I'm going where I'll trouble you no more - and I'll be troubled no more. Now do you know ... And if the police are looking for my body, tell 'em to go to the old brickworks pond and drop their grappling irons in at the deep end - and if they fish long enough they'll come up with something. And then you can pay all your bloody neighbours out of the insurance policies you've got locked away in your trunk -

HARRY exits with the air of a man about to do something desperate.

During scene change bring up sound of CHILDREN's voices, singing street songs.

* * *

ACT ONE   Scene Three

Street

JACK HARWOOD enters carrying length
of hosepipe over shoulder, and ALBERT
KIPPAX enters carrying knapsack.

ALBERT   Howdy Jack! - where are tha off - going to swill thyself
down?

JACK   Nar, it's for Polly.

ALBERT   Oh, I see ... she needs   cooling down.

JACK   Nah, I mean for doing the backyard. Where are you off?

ALBERT   Allotment. I'm gettin' some maggots. I've got a dead
cat rottin'.

JACK   Aye there's been a few missin' lately.

ALBERT   I'm goin' off for a day's fishin' tomorrow.

JACK   Anything to get away from the house.

ALBERT   That's it. I can't stand the tension, see - Beatty an' mi
Mother, see.

JACK   Polly's just as bad with her Mother.

ALBERT   Aye, women seem to thrive on a bit of conflict. Yet if
you stick your nose in they'll both turn on you.

JACK   They're all off their bloody heads, if you ask me. Here,
mate, have a smoke. But you've got to go with 'em - never
go against 'um. That's what I've found out.

He holds out packet with one cigarette.

ALBERT   Nay, I can't take thy last one.

JACK   Let's share it then. I've smoked three this last half an
hour. I go bloody mad once I let myself go.

JACK breaks cigarette in two and
gives ALBERT half, puts the other
between his own lips, and ALBERT
lights them both.

ALBERT   And I'll go mad if I don't get back down pit again soon.

JACK   Know what, I wouldn't care if I never saw the bottom of a
                coal mine again.

ALBERT   Never saw the bottom of the pit again - tha'rt codding!

JACK   I'm not. What - going off from thy own fireside six
                nights out of seven: waiting for trams in all bloody
                weathers: often soaked to the skin and all huddled wet
                through together going down in the cage. And the bloody
                winder is so rough, that if tha takes milk it's bloody
                butter when tha gets down. Aye, these weeks at home
                have opened my eyes. What's the big attraction in slaving
                away at the coalface in thy underpants with the bloody
                sweat pouring off thee?

ALBERT   I wear an old pair of Beatty's knickers.

JACK   Keep it dark!

ALBERT   Aye, I ripped my pants one day, so I put hers on.
                They're very comfortable.

JACK   I dare say they're more roomy.

ALBERT   They seem to bring her close to me when I'm wearing 'em.
                Oh, but I'm longing to get a pick or a shovel back into my
                hands, and start grafting and feeling the sweat pouring
                out of me once more.

JACK   Get off!

ALBERT   I'll tell you what it is - I never had a job that made me
                sweat till I went down the mine. I were what they call
                delicate, see - and my mam swore she'd never let me go
                down pit. I started work at twelve in the spinning - but
                the minute I went through the spinning room door it were
                that hot I bloody collapsed. Flat on my face and they
                had to carry me out. Then my Uncle Charlie got me a
                job with him at the glass works as an apprentice glass-
                blower. I used to run out of breath halfway through - I'd
                asthma, see.

JACK   Tha musta ruined some bloody bottles.

ALBERT   I did. Firm nearly went flamin' bankrupt. So they got
shut of me. I had job after job - I worked at the tannery
for a time, and I stank that much from all those hides
that nobody would sit near me. I used to have to walk
home, because if I got on a full tram it bloody emptied in
two minutes. Aye, I kept asking my mam could I go down
pit with my dad but she wouldn't let me. Neither would
he. So one day I went to Brackley Pit an' got took on on
my own. First they knew was when I came home all
black.

JACK   They say if it's in the blood it'll come out.

ALBERT   For the first few shifts I thought I'd never be able to keep
going. I used to be soaked in sweat afore t'others even
started. My guts were that sore I felt sick all the time.
Dusta know, I used to be that weak when I got home from
the afternoon shift, I couldn't eat a thing. My mam used
to make me a bowl of gruel - it was all I could get down.
Her used to have tears in her eyes, watching me. Chuck
the pit in, love, she used to say - find a job on top. Get
yourself out of that Plodder mine.

JACK   Aye, I worked in the Plodder one time - under an eighteen
inch roof. Even bloody mice were bowlegged.

ALBERT   Often when I'd turn over my clog toe 'ud get stuck against
a low part of the roof. And sometimes when I were lying
on my back, scrawping away with the pick, my e'een full
of sweat, my mouth full of coal dust, and my arms
dropping off, the only way I could keep going was to say,
"Albert, it's not thee, it's some other bugger."

JACK   And tha' wants to get back to that lot!

ALBERT   Aye, I do for sure. Once I got the upper hand on the
job it were marvellous. I came to realise tha can do
owt if tha keeps at it.   I got as I used to come out of
that pithead feeling like a bloody lion let loose. I hadn't
a care in the world. Now they reckon that if the pumpmen
don't go back the pits'll be flooded.

JACK   Take no notice, that's only newspaper talk to frighten us
back.

ALBERT   You know what, Jack, I could bloody cry when I think of
what the miners have done for their country, my Dad and
my three brothers - and now see how the country is treatin
the miners.

JACK | One thing I've learnt, Albert - if they bloody need you they'll pay you, and if they don't they damn well won't . It's as simple as that.

> Enter from other side of stage
> OLIVE, BEATTY and FANNY,
> chatting and carrying stools and
> chairs to sit on.

FANNY | I say, just look at reflection of setting sun across on yon factory windows. Isn't it a bonny sight.

OLIVE | You could paint a picture of it.

BEATTY | Ay, if you'd any flamin' paint! (Calls across to ALBERT) Hey, have you not gone for your maggots yet.

ALBERT | I'm just going.

JACK | I think I'd best be off too. Polly will be waiting for this hosepipe.

ALBERT | (to JACK) So long.

JACK | So long, Albert. I'll be seeing thee.

> JACK exits and ALBERT goes
> across to the WOMEN.

ALBERT | (to OLIVE and FANNY) Hello, there.

FANNY | Hello, Jack love.

OLIVE | Hello.

ALBERT | Well, I'll be off. (Whispers to BEATTY) Was my mum all right?

BEATTY | Yes - why?

ALBERT | You'll be sure to go into her.

BEATTY | Course I will. I always do. You're more worried about your mother than you are about your own wife and son.

ALBERT | I know you'll look after him, but she's not been herself lately. Goodbye.

BEATTY | Ta ra.

Ad lib ta ra's. ALBERT exits.

BEATTY   Did you hear him - "Be sure to go in to my Mother?"

FANNY   It's a good fault in a man to love his own Mother.

OLIVE   (to BEATTY) Aye, Beatty. You might be glad of it your-
                self one day.

FANNY   You stifle somebody's affection - it doesn't matter what
                it's for - and it turns sour.

                        LIZ SEDWIN hurries across behind
                        them, wearing a coat.

                Hello, Liz.

                        LIZ waves and hurries off.

                You'll speak when your money's done.

BEATTY   That's funny, Liz Sedwin leaving the shop of an evening.
                I wonder where she's off.

OLIVE   There's something very peculiar going on at Sedwin's.
                I've got some winnings to collect on the Derby and I'm
                getting nervous - they haven't started paying out yet.

FANNY   You never need worry where Liz Sedwin's concerned.

OLIVE   It's not her I worry about, it's him - and the winnings
                aren't just for myself. I've a lot of folk to pay out.

FANNY   No gossip about Liz. She's helped half the street out of
                their troubles and got no thanks ...

                        FANNY gives a groan and holds
                        bottom of her back.

BEATTY   What's up with you?

FANNY   I just felt a funny pain in the bottom of my back.

BEATTY   I expect you've got a touch of lumbago.

OLIVE   More like it's a sympathy pain with your Polly.

FANNY	Our Polly! - I don't want to hear anything about her. We just met face to face in Sedwin's and ... (She stoops her face in her hands and stifles a sob)
OLIVE	Now then, Fanny, don't take it to heart.
FANNY	What else can I do? I'm a fool, I know I'm a fool! And what hurts most I know the very thing inside her that makes her do it to me.
BEATTY	I expect it's like watching your own self in your daughter.
OLIVE	(gives BEATTY a look and glibly changes subject) Here, talking about pain reminds me of last night in bed. It must have been about 1 o'clock. My left knee were warching me and I couldn't sleep, so I woke yon fellow up and asked him to rub it. "Didn't the infirmary doctor say not to rub it?" he said.
BEATTY	Any excuse not to get up. That's men all over.
FANNY	I wish I had my husband to be next to - I wouldn't mind what pain I had.
BEATTY	I suppose you miss 'em when they're gone. Did you get him to rub it?
OLIVE	Course I did. After all, I'm bringing the money into the home. I don't say owt - but he knows - in fact the kids know, and I've to see they don't take advantage.
BEATTY	Aye, you don't have the same respect if a man's not earning.
OLIVE	No, but I still serve him first at table.
FANNY	Did it shift it?
OLIVE	No, but it took me mind off it and that's the main thing. I mean, I couldn't bear the idea he was sleeping and I wasn't. Ee, but it was all I could do to keep a straight face, seeing him knelt there in his little short shirt, rubbing away at my knee. They're such ugly beggars are men, when you come to weigh 'em up at close quarters.
BEATTY	We don't marry 'em for their beauty.

The trio find all this very funny.

OLIVE	We'd be hard up if we did.
FANNY	I can remember like it was only yesterday the very first afternoon Gilbert came home from the pit in his dirt.
OLIVE	Aye, God rest him - it's surprising how many faces you miss round this street.
BEATTY	(to FANNY) Go on Fanny.
FANNY	We'd been married three days like, we just went to Morecambe for the week-end for our honeymoon.
BEATTY	Not much of a honeymoon!
FANNY	It were long enough for us! We didn't know how to pass the time.
OLIVE	Aye, it is a problem.
FANNY	It was out of season, you see.
BEATTY	Well, it does make a difference.
OLIVE	And he was a shy lad was Gilbert.
FANNY	Until he got to know you, then he could be the other way about. Anyway, we'd got our own little home together, nothing to boast about - but everything our own.
BEATTY	That must be lovely.
FANNY	I thought it was. There wasn't a happier lass in the land. Anyway, he was on the day shift - had left home at half-past four that morning, and at three in the afternoon I was listening for his clogs along the street. His Mother told me they appreciate it if you're there to open the door.
OLIVE	Aye, a sort of welcome.
FANNY	Yes, but no fuss.
BEATTY	And don't talk to 'em too much.
FANNY	He came in the door all black, just his teeth showing, and the whites of his eyes. We just smiled at one another like I could see he was weary - and he tramped through into the kitchen and took his clogs off. He washed his hands under the tap and then splashed his lips and then came in front

FANNY (Cont)	place and sat down and ate his dinner in his pit dirt. When he'd supped his mug of tea after it, he got up and he says, "Fanny, I think I'll just curl me up on the hearth-rug in front of fire and have five minutes snooze before I wash me." "Oh no you won't," I says, "You'll wash you first." I didn't like saying it, but his Mother had warned me, see. "If you once start letting him sleep in his dirt in front of the hearth the home will never be your own. I've had twenty seven years of his Dad doing it. They get down on that rug and they go out like a dead horse. You can't get next or near fireplace for your baking or anything. Then when they waken up, you can't get 'em to go and wash in a draughty cold kitchen. They want to wash in front of the fire, and you won't find it in your heart to refuse 'em. Your floor gets messed up and you're never done carrying water from one place to another. Course, they're that stupefied with work and weariness they don't realise the trouble they're causing you. So you put your foot down at the start - as soon as he's finished his dinner, make him go in the back kitchen and wash him. He'll get it over all the more quickly in the cold kitchen, and then when he wants to sleep he can go upstairs to bed out of the way. All the young wives of today are doing that. And they certainly won't scrub their husbands down on the rug." So Gilbert looked at me and looked at the fire and the rug, and then went into the kitchen to wash him. I'd a big iron pot of water heating on the hob and I carried it in and poured it into the enamel wash basin I'd set on the slops stone. Then I came in and closed the door and started warming the towel in front of the fire. I could hear him puffing and blowing away as he was washing, but I didn't go in.
BEATTY	Why not?
FANNY	I was a bit shy of seeing a chap in his bare skin.
OLIVE	Ee, but you'd been on your honeymoon together, hadn't you?
BEATTY	You must have slept in the same bed.
FANNY	Aye, but he'd had his shirt on - I mean, we're not savages.
	Laughter.
OLIVE	The things we women could tell!

FANNY	Well, the next thing I heard him call, "Fanny, will you come and give my back a scrub?" I felt a bit nervous, but I went into the kitchen and there he was, standing two-doubled over the wash bowl. So I stood there behind him for a minute and looked at his back, and it seemed so broad and strong it looked like a a great lump of black granite. I didn't know how to start on it.
OLIVE	Poor you.
FANNY	So I picks up wet flannel and soaps it and starts quietly washing him. "That'll never do," says Gilbert. "You'll have to use the scrubbing brush. My Mum always did." So I picks up scrubbing brush, a new one it was, and the bristles were that hard I was frightened of using it properly. "That's no use," he says, "you'll have to lay it on a bit or else you'll never get the dirt off." So I started scrubbing. "That's better," he grunts. "That's how mi mum always did it." So when I'd got all the dirt out, I picked up the flannel and began to wipe him clean, then suddenly for the first time I saw his naked back. I'll never forget the sight.
OLIVE	Why - what was wrong with it, love?
FANNY	It was one great mass of cuts and bruises and little blue scars.
BEATTY	That's what they get working on the coal face.
FANNY	I filled up at the sight, you know. I mean it told me so much. Course, I didn't let him see -
OLIVE	No, he wouldn't have thanked you.
BEATTY	They don't like pity.
FANNY	I'd a sudden little impulse to bend down and kiss one great sore weal across his back - but I managed to stop myself.
BEATTY	He'd have wondered what was up.
FANNY	Anyway, when he'd finished his top part, I lifted the bowl on to the floor and helped him wash his legs and that. He didn't say anything, but he seemed a bit surprised I should help him. It would never have struck me a minute before, but that back had brought me so much closer to him, you see. Then as I was drying him down with the towel, I said, casual like, "Gilbert, if you'd rather wash

FANNY (Cont)	in front of the fire I don't mind at all. Or if it's more comfy to have a little sleep on the rug first, you please yourself. It's no trouble to me."
OLIVE	You've got to make it up to them one way or another.
BEATTY	If the wife doesn't, who will? That's what we're here for. I'd best go in and see how old Sarah is ...

BEATTY exits.

Creep in soft distant singing of
children - "Poor Jenny is a 'weeping".

OLIVE	You know what, Fanny, it's hard to believe it's five years ago since the morning they brought you that War Office telegram.
FANNY	Five years! - it seems like an eternity to me. And do you know - there are times when I lie awake and think of him, and I can't bring his face to mind, but often in the middle of the night the one thing I can remember is his back, as it looked that first day, stooped over the kitchen sink.

OLIVE and FANNY sit there thoughtfully
as the children's song is heard.
Suddenly they both turn as BEATTY re-
enters in a breathless, almost hysterical
state.

BEATTY	(nearly speechless) Oh ... come ... come ... Olive - Fanny - quick ...

OLIVE and FANNY jump up. BEATTY
tries to speak again.

OLIVE	What's up, love?
FANNY	What is it? Calm yourself!
BEATTY	It's ... it's old Sarah ... she's ... she's ... she's ...

OLIVE and FANNY look aghast as they
sense bad news.

CURTAIN FALLS

(During interval the children's singing
continues)

ACT TWO   Scene One

The curtain rises on the KIPPAX FRONT
KITCHEN.

OLIVE and FANNY are stooped anxiously
over a figure in the rocking-chair, which
they are masking by their ministrations.

FANNY   Ee, the poor thing - she feels ice cold ...

OLIVE   (feeling) Aye, she's like death. Who'd have thought it!
Rub her hands, Fanny.

FANNY   That's what I am doing ... can't you see ... but it's not
making much difference.

OLIVE   Y'aven't got any smelling salts handy, have you.

FANNY   What do you think I am, walking around with smelling
salts ... Oh, what shall we do!

OLIVE and FANNY turn as SARAH
enters carrying a cup of water. We
now see that it is BEATTY in the
chair.

SARAH   Here, fling this cold water over her - that'll fetch her
round.

OLIVE takes cup.

OLIVE   Ta. D'you think it's right?

SARAH   Course it's right.

OLIVE looks at cup then looks at
BEATTY. She makes as if to throw
then stops.

Ee, I can't bring myself to do it.

SARAH   Give it me then! I'll fetch her round!

SARAH takes cup back from OLIVE.
BEATTY is seen to move.

FANNY   Steady up there, she's coming round.

BEATTY comes round.

BEATTY	Did I go over?
FANNY	Yes, but you're all right now.
OLIVE	(looks at cup) You're just in time, Beatty.
SARAH	Only just!

SARAH turns to put cup down.

BEATTY	(furiously to SARAH) Oh, you - I could ... it's all your fault ... (To OLIVE and FANNY) I'm right sorry.
FANNY	It's all right, love.
OLIVE	Don't worry - we quite understand ... you got a shock.
BEATTY	I got two shocks not one. (Angrily to SARAH) First I thought -
SARAH	You thought what?
BEATTY	Oh, I could ... How often have I told you not to go to sleep on that chair with your teeth out!
SARAH	What have you got so upset about? They're my teeth, and they're paid for, and I'll do with them as I think fit.
BEATTY	(to FANNY and OLIVE) Ee, but I'm right sorry - she frightened the life out of me, yu'know.
SARAH	You didn't want for me to leave 'em in an' choke my flamin' self did you?
FANNY	Now quiet yourself, Sarah.
OLIVE	Aye, calm down.
SARAH	I am calm. It's you lot look ruffled. What's all the fuss about anyway?
BEATTY	The way she lay back in that chair with her cheeks all sunk in and her mouth wide open, I could have sworn she were dead. That's why I ran out.
SARAH	You mean you hoped I was dead.

BEATTY   What a terrible thing to say!

OLIVE   I'm surprised at you, Sarah.

FANNY   Sarah, that's not like you.

SARAH   Not that I'd blame her.

BEATTY   You shouldn't have said that.

SARAH   They say the wish is never far behind the thought.

FANNY   Well, it was in this case.

OLIVE   Of course it was, the poor girl couldn't have been more
                upset if it had been her own mother.   Why, you're looking
                that well, Sarah, I reckon they'll have to take you out and
                shoot you.

SARAH   Well, I only wish somebody would - and the sooner the
                flamin' better, for what use I am.

FANNY   That's not like you, Sarah, giving way to your feelings.

OLIVE   I'm surprised at her talking like that - this is her lucky
                day. Don't you know!

SARAH   I don't think I'll ever know another lucky day as long as I
                live.

FANNY   Eeh! Shame on you.

OLIVE   Now don't you lose heart, Sarah.

                        Enter ALBERT KIPPAX with fishing
                        bag. He is taken aback.

ALBERT   What's going on here?

FANNY   Hello, Albert love.

OLIVE   You're back, Albert! We're just going.

FANNY   We only looked in.

ALBERT   Why ... what's up?

BEATTY   It's your Mum again.

SARAH	Hello, love.
ALBERT	Hello Mam. Are you all right?
SARAH	Course I'm all right. Why?
ALBERT	Nothing wrong, is there?
SARAH	No. Did you get your maggots?
ALBERT	No. Somebody had pinched the dead cat.
SARAH	Aye, you can't leave anything around these days.
ALBERT	(to BEATTY) What about mi Mum?
BEATTY	I came in and found her lying there with her mouth open and I thought -
SARAH	She thought I'd snuffed it. But she were mistaken - more or less.
FANNY	It was a simple mistake, Albert. Beatty called us for help.
OLIVE	That's right. I think we'd best be off.
FANNY	Aye, come on, Olive. Goodbye. So long, Sarah.
SARAH	Thanks for reviving me!
OLIVE	I'll be calling in to see you, Sarah.
SARAH	What about?
OLIVE	As if you didn't know! Cheerio.

Exit OLIVE and FANNY.

SARAH	I wonder what she wants to call around for.
ALBERT	You haven't been out in the street for a breath of fresh air, Mum. Like you promised you would.
SARAH	Somehow I didn't fancy it when it came to it. I couldn't work up the enthusiasm. Besides, who'd want to listen to me.

ALBERT   I'm sure you'd feel better if you mixed a bit more with the neighbours like you used to do, and talked things out of yourself.

BEATTY   Yes. She should try and make a bit more effort. Not doze off in her chair with her teeth out.

SARAH   Aye, I'll put my white nightie on next time - then if I do kick the bucket it won't be no trouble to lay me out.

BEATTY   Can you hear her!

ALBERT   Shall I make you some pobs, mam?

BEATTY   There's not enough milk for pobs. We'll need most of it for Wellington's night feed.

ALBERT   We'll make do. He won't starve.

                    Exit BEATTY into kitchen.

SARAH   Don't bother. I'm not really hungry, love. I don't know what's come over me. I'm just a flamin' nuisance to myself and everybody else. I'd never have thought it would come to this.

ALBERT   Would you like me to get you a basin of that soup they're doling out at the Ram's Head?

SARAH   Nay, there's no free soup coming into this home.

ALBERT   Don't be ashamed of being hungry, Mam.

SARAH   I'm not. But I'd be ashamed of folk knowing. If there's one thing I detest it's pity. Besides, you only make them feel uncomfortable.

ALBERT   Suppose I make you a cup of tea? Now what about that, Mam?

SARAH   I don't suppose it has owt to do with food or drink. It seems a sort of emptiness of heart. I'll go and sleep it away. It'll come right - all in God's good time.

ALBERT   You can't go to sleep at this hour.

SARAH   I'm getting as I can go to sleep at any hour. There's times when I scarcely know the difference. I feel neither here nor there.

ALBERT   Don't talk like that, Mam.

SARAH   No I mustn't, or they'll be sending me away.

ALBERT   Sending you away! Where to?

SARAH   You know.

ALBERT   Nobody'll send you away whilst I'm around.

SARAH   There's one or two old 'uns gone from this street as I
            know of. They'd lived here sixty years or more - and
            they got rid of 'um in a few minutes. Course you can't
            blame the young 'uns - they have their lives to live and
            I'm not all that gone on old folk myself. We are a pest -
            hanging on like we do.

ALBERT   Hush, mum. You mustn't talk like that.

SARAH   You'd never have me sent away to one of those places,
            would you, love?

ALBERT   Don't be silly. Course I wouldn't.

SARAH   They all promise you that, but when you become a nuisance
            they soon get rid of you. They get you to sign one of those
            forms and before you know where you are the yellow cab's
            at the door and they're all kissing you goodbye an' telling
            you how kind the nurses are and what a nice time you'll
            have. Mind you, it's not that I worry about the hardship,
            I've had plenty of that, it's the loneliness I couldn't stand.
            Somehow I can't get used to new folk and strange surroundings
            at my age. I was born in this street and I'd like to die in it.

ALBERT   And I'll see you do, Mother - but please God that won't be
            for a long time yet. And you must forgive me if at times I
            can't do all I would for you.

                    Enter BEATTY. She crosses to cot.

SARAH   It's all right, I understand, love. You've always been a good
            son to me, so don't worry yourself, I know things are not
            easy for you - you're pulled one way and another with mother
            and wife under the one roof. It's not fair to you. Not to
            either of you. Look, if ever you really want me out of the
            way, love - I'll go. I will honest. I might even be happy in
            one of them institutions.

ALBERT   Mother, please don't talk like that.

SARAH   Well, I'll get off. Goodnight.

ALBERT   Well, good night, mum, and God Bless.

SARAH   Good night, Beatty.

BEATTY   Goodnight.

SARAH   (to BEATTY) I'm sorry about what I said and how I went
                on. I get like that at times.

BEATTY   It's all right this time - but try an' control yourself in
                future.

                        SARAH exits.

                        ALBERT looks unhappily after his
                        MOTHER. BEATTY decides to pull
                        his attention back to herself, and she
                        approaches him intimately and gives
                        him a kiss that has a promise of sex.

BEATTY   Let's get off early tonight, Albert. Shall we?

ALBERT   Get off where?

BEATTY   To bed. Where do you think.

                        BEATTY snuggles close to ALBERT.

ALBERT   Now don't come that game.

BEATTY   What game?

ALBERT   You know, getting at me like that. I'm sorry - but it
                won't work.

BEATTY   (huffed) Don't be so unpleasant about it. I did it for
                your sake more than mine.

ALBERT   How d'you mean - for my sake.

BEATTY   Well, I thought it would take your mind off things. Being
                as you've been so stand-offish lately.

ALBERT I don't want my mind taking off things - not that way.

BEATTY What other way is there - the state we're in? It's
the only bit of pleasure going.

ALBERT Don't talk like that, Beatty - you know I don't like it.
I haven't given up yet, and I won't sink to that level.

BEATTY What level?

ALBERT I wouldn't like to think that when we - when we came
together, like, we were only doing it because we couldn't
afford to go to the pictures. Have you any money? I'd
love to get my mother something nice.

BEATTY I have got her two ounces of best butter. I was saving it
for her toast in the morning.

ALBERT I meant something substantial.

BEATTY I can only do my best. Do you realize she lost her last
shilling on the Derby?

ALBERT I suppose it gave her a bit of hope.

BEATTY She's getting very awkward lately.

ALBERT You don't handle her right.

BEATTY How should I handle her?

ALBERT You go around making her feel she's in the way.

BEATTY Well, she is in the way.

ALBERT Don't let me hear you say that again. She's not in my
way.

BEATTY Well, she's in my way. And she resents having me
around.

ALBERT She doesn't. It's just that she's always had her own way
of doing things, and it's hard for her to change.

BEATTY And she's jealous of my child.

ALBERT She's not jealous - but you make such a fuss over him you
give nobody else a chance. You should see her with him when
you're not here.

          The raised voices waken the baby
          and it cries. BEATTY goes to it.

BEATTY   Hush, love.

ALBERT   At times you use him to get your own way.

BEATTY   You don't realise what I've got to go through with her
when you're out of the way. She sits there talking to
herself.

ALBERT   What do you expect, for Godsake! She's brought four
of us up in this little house. She used to be up at half-
past-four of a morning and it'd be midnight before she
got to bed, cooking, cleaning and washing. You've
no idea what work it is for a woman looking after four
sons in a little place like this. I've seen her have a standup
fight with our Jimmy getting him up for bit of a morning.
She never had a minute to herself and now she doesn't know
how to fill in her time. No wonder she talks to herself.

BEATTY   If I had my way I could do something with this place.
I'd get rid of all the old stuff and make it modern -
once you're back working.

ALBERT   Bear in mind that she's not living with us, we're
living with her. She and my Dad came into this house
the day they got married. She's spent endless hours
over the years scrubbing, washing and polishing in this
room, and her bits of furniture mean everything to her.

BEATTY   They might to her but they don't to me. I want my own
home. Another thing, I don't like saying this, but
she doesn't look after herself like she should.

ALBERT   She might not have the same pride in herself, but she's
very clean. And though she might seem a useless old
woman to you, don't forget to me she's my mother.

BEATTY   I understand that.

ALBERT   I can't bear to think of the change that's come over her
these past years. She used to have these rosy cheeks,
bonny arms - I can see her this minute as she used to be,
stooped over the dolly tub on washdays, rubbing and
scrubbing away, and she'd be singing as she was hanging her
clothes out to dry in the back. And her word carried
weight in this street. They used to come for Mum when
there was trouble amongst the neighbours, if anybody was

ALBERT (Cont)	ill or dying, they'd come for her to help out, and in those days the women always wanted her to attend with the mid-wife when they were having a baby. They said she gave 'em confidence.

> The baby has gone quiet. BEATTY tidies cot and stands up.

BEATTY	I'm not saying she hadn't had her troubles - the same as anybody else.

> ALBERT opens a drawer and takes out a box and opens it.

ALBERT	She's seen three of her sons go out of that door and all she's got left of em are these. Our Frank's watch, our Sammy's flute, our Jimmy's first clogs. You're a mother yourself. You have some idea what that can do to a woman.

> There is a moment of understanding from BEATTY

BEATTY	I'm sorry, Albert. Somehow I never quite understood till this minute. Do forgive me.

> BEATTY approaches ALBERT. For a moment they are uncertain, then ALBERT takes her into his arms with tenderness, and then with some force he kisses her.

> Enter, outside front door, OLIVE, and she walks in eagerly, tapping as she does.

OLIVE	It's only me again. (She sees ALBERT and BEATTY break away) Oh, do excuse me ...

> ALBERT and BEATTY are full of embarrassment.

BEATTY	It's all right ...
OLIVE	I could come back later ...
ALBERT	It's all right - what is it?
OLIVE	I mean I don't want to put anybody off anything ...
ALBERT	(incensed) You're putting nobody off! What is it?

OLIVE   I mean there's not enough of that going on in this
street - if you ask me.

BEATTY   Olive, what is it?

OLIVE   Will you tell Sarah, I'm just off to draw her winnings ...

BEATTY   What winnings?

OLIVE   She backed Humorist - six to one - she's seven bob to
come back ...

ALBERT   I'll call her ...

              ALBERT exits to back kitchen, calling.

              Mam! Mam! Some good news for you!

OLIVE   (to BEATTY) I'm glad to see your courting days are
not over!

BEATTY   He was only -

OLIVE   It doesn't matter what he was doing - but you keep him
up to it -- giving you the odd hug and kiss during the day -
they come from the heart, see - and they beat a bloody
bagful of the sort you get at night ...

              Bring up sound of children singing, off.

                   * * *

ACT TWO Scene Two

SEDWIN'S SHOP

                  LIZ SEDWIN enters from kitchen. She has
just returned, and is wearing the fresh
blouse she put on to go borrowing. She
looks quite attractive. She carries a tin
with silver and notes in, and the betting
slips. She puts them down on the counter
and begins to reckon what there is to pay out,
marking the amount on each slip.

LIZ   Humorist, threepence win, at six to one, one and ninepence to come ... (Marks it) Humorist, shilling win ...
at six to one, seven shillings to come (Marks it) ...

                  HARRY enters quietly from the street.
LIZ realises he is there but doesn't
look up.

            ... Humorist, threepence each way ... (Dead casual:
never looks up) I thought you'd gone off to drown
yourself ...

HARRY   I had.

LIZ   Threepence win brings one-and-nine, threepence place,
at quarter odds, plus stakes, brings ...

HARRY   Tenpence ha'penny. Two-and-sevenpence ha'penny to
come back.

LIZ   Thank you.

HARRY   Pay to the nearest penny. Oh the bookies' side.

LIZ   I'll pay in full, if you don't mind. (Speaks as she writes)
Two and sevenpence ha'penny. (Picks up, casual) And what
happened?

HARRY   I changed my mind. I got there ... put mi finger in the
water ... and thought I'd put it off till August.

LIZ   What a pity ... (Continues to sort out slips)

HARRY   (sweetly) Yes, isn't it. The thought came over me - why
go out of your way just to please a gaggle of bloody women.
And since you've come out of worse scrapes you'll come out
of this one -

LIZ   That's what you think!

                          HARRY has been watching LIZ and now
                          stealthily approaches her, lovingly,
                          his skilful arm slipping round her waist.

HARRY   Now then, Liz love ...

                          LIZ makes fierce grab and picks up
                          carving knife - and raises it in front
                          of her. HARRY jumps back with alarm.

LIZ   If you so much as put a finger near me ...

                          LIZ and HARRY are facing each other.
                          OLIVE enters and sees them. Looks
                          are exchanged. HARRY takes knife as
                          though LIZ has been inspecting it.

HARRY   Yes, Liz, you're right ... I'll sharpen it in the morning.

OLIVE   It's me again!

HARRY   We can see that.

                          LIZ is all smiles at OLIVE.

OLIVE   I've come to draw my winnings.

                          HARRY puts knife down and takes over
                          tin of money with air of authority.

HARRY   Winnings ... certainly ... (Jingles money in tin loudly)
                   Have you got the counterfoils?

OLIVE   The what!

HARRY   Your copies of the bets! I want to know what I'm paying
                   out.

OLIVE   I've got all the initials, and the amounts written down ...

HARRY   Carry on ...

                          LIZ has picked up the carving knife and
                          is trying the blade with her thumb. She
                          seems possessed of a strong desire to
                          use it on HARRY.

OLIVE   O. W. - that's me -

HARRY   Yes, always get yourself in first - how much?

OLIVE   Five an' three to come.

HARRY   O. W. Five an' three, correct.

OLIVE   S. K. - that's Sarah Kippax.

HARRY   Seven shillings. Here, gimme your paper - I'll do 'em
         all in no time.

         HARRY takes paper and checks up
         rapidly.

OLIVE   (sweetly) It's nice to hear of someone winning for a
         change.

LIZ   Yes, isn't it.

HARRY   (muttering and reckoning) You've four pounds eighteen
         and ninepence to come in all.

OLIVE   (amazed) That's right ... everybody in the mill backed
         it. Four pounds, eighteen and ninepence ha'penny, I
         made it.

HARRY   We don't pay odd ha'pennies.

LIZ   (cuts in) Give the customer her ha'penny.

         HARRY hands money over, counting it
         clearly for OLIVE, and adds ha'penny
         with an extra flourish.

HARRY   Four pounds, eighteen and ninepence ha'penny.

OLIVE   Ta ... I had an awful feeling I wasn't going to get
         paid ...

HARRY   Sedwin always pays ... always has ... always will ...

LIZ   (aside) Aye, if somebody finds him the money.

OLIVE   Hy - you're a shilling short.

HARRY   (too quickly) Am I! Oh, sorry. (Hands her shilling)

OLIVE   First one I'll pay is Sarah Kippax ... ta ra ...

HARRY   Goodbye ...

LIZ   So long, Olive ...

                    OLIVE exits. LIZ has taken to feeling
                    at the carving knife blade again.

HARRY   Put that down, Liz.

LIZ   You know what I'd like to do to you ...

HARRY   You'd only waken up sometime in the middle of the night
             and feel sorry for it. Where'd you get the money?

LIZ   (bitter resignation) I parted with something very dear to
             me ... but at least I'll be able to hold my head up in the
             street. But let me tell you - you've done with this book-
             making runner game - there's not another betting slip coming
             into this shop. Tomorrow morning at seven o'clock you'll
             get out of bed and go and look for some proper work.

                    HARRY starts coughing.

HARRY   Look for work! Why if it weren't for my malaria, I could
             be working as a navvy ganger.

LIZ   I don't believe you've ever had malaria. You might cod
             the M.O. , but you'll never cod me.

HARRY   (coughing) Because I'm codding some of the time doesn't
             mean I'm coddin' all of the bloody time.

LIZ   Any mosquito as bit you would be damn hard up. But
             you've been on this swindling game for weeks - what have
             you been doing with the money?

HARRY   Nothing.

LIZ   I suppose you've been playing the big I-am in the pub,
             treating all your hangers-on.

HARRY   I've stood my corner amongst my mates same as I've
             always done.

LIZ   You and your flamin' mates. That's all you men think
             of - your mates. You never think of your home.

HARRY	I think of a lot of things I say nothing about.
LIZ	Or happen you've got yourself some fancy woman tucked away somewhere on the quiet. I wouldn't put it past you.
HARRY	You know that's never been one of my weaknesses, Liz.
LIZ	Pity help her if you have, for what use you'd be. She'd be on a damn poor wicket, waiting for the innings that never comes.
HARRY	That wasn't what you said when I came on furlough that time and I took you to mi Uncle Dick's at Matlock - was it?
LIZ	You mean your big weekend - your Indian Summer. You've never done patting yourself on the back over that lot. It must have been the Derbyshire mountain air, or all that bully beef you'd been eating.

HARRY sneaks up intimately against
LIZ.

HARRY	Do you remember the afternoon we climbed on to that haystack, Liz?
LIZ	I've told you keep your mitts off me. What haystack?
HARRY	You know! I remember you were wearing that gingham dress I used to like you in, all puckered in at the waist with a full skirt. Then afterwards we fell asleep with the sun shining down on our faces. Then I remember when I woke up you were putting my puttees back on for me.
LIZ	I musta been outa my flamin' mind.
HARRY	I'd never seen 'em looking so spruce in all my service. Then after you'd fastened 'em you looked up and kissed me and said, "Aahe, my bonny young gamecock!"

HARRY puts arm round LIZ. LIZ pushes
him away.

LIZ	Take your great big dirty maulers away! If I did - I've never had cause to say it again, have I? Gamecock .. huh ... !
HARRY	I wonder did you fasten my puttees too tight, Liz, and shut off the circulation.

LIZ	I must have shut something off! You've never been the same man since. Course they do say, Nature gelds you and never tells you.
HARRY	Well, it hasn't done it to me yet! ... But with this flamin' shop on your mind night and day, I never get a chance to woo you ...
LIZ	You! You couldn't woo our ...

> LIZ stops as ALBERT KIPPAX enters in his quiet way.

LIZ	Oh, hello, Albert.
ALBERT	(smiles) Beatty said you'd some lovely roast heart - have you any left?

> ALBERT brings out plate from under his jacket.

HARRY	(cuts in) Aye ... all the bloody lot.
LIZ	I'll get it, love.

> LIZ gives HARRY a look and exits.

HARRY	How's married life going?
ALBERT	Quite fair ... at times.
HARRY	Well, you'll find, Albert, the longer you're wed, the fewer and farther between those bloody times become.

> JACK HARWOOD enters, looking worried.

You here again! What's it to be this time.

> ALBERT and JACK ad lib 'howdo's'.

JACK	Have you a bottle of Waddicor's quick drying varnish?

> LIZ enters carrying roast heart, which she puts on counter.

Polly wants me to varnish the chairs in case we have any visitors.

HARRY   You're going to have a visitor all right ... better get
your running pumps on to go for the midwife.

> LIZ picks up a bundle of large white
> sheets of paper off the counter, and
> rolls them up in a thick roll.

LIZ   Forget the varnish, love. Take her this thick paper.

> JACK is mystified and ALBERT is
> interested in the whole thing.

JACK   But what for!

LIZ   She'll know soon enough. Go on.

JACK   But what'll I tell her?

HARRY   You don't have to tell her anything. You're only the
flamin' father. Go on - imshi!

> JACK exits with paper.

LIZ   (sharply to HARRY) Language!

ALBERT   Beatty said there were sage and onion stuffing as well.

HARRY   Don't worry - it's inside - you'll get your share.

LIZ   How much were you thinking of, love - quarter, half-a-
pound, or what ...

ALBERT   Mi Mother said go lavish - she's had a win on the Derby.

HARRY   Aye - we heard all about it.

> LIZ gives HARRY a look then turns to
> the heart.

LIZ   (to ALBERT) Shall we say half-a-pound, then ...

ALBERT   Start cutting, and I'll tell you better as you go on.

> LIZ is about to start cutting when she
> gets this feeling that it's all not worth
> bothering about, and an idea crosses
> her mind.

LIZ   Why don't you take the lot ... eh, love - ?

ALBERT   (astonished)   The lot ... you mean the full roast heart ..
just as it is!   But how much will all that cost!

HARRY   Here, have it on the bloody house ... it's one of them day

                 HARRY puts whole heart on ALBERT's plate,
                 thrusts it into his hands, and pushes him out.

     ... imshi ... iggeri!

LIZ   Don't use those filthy Arabic words in my shop.

HARRY   It only means push off.

                 HARRY turns to LIZ with air of masterful
                 lover.

     - now ... what were you saying I couldn't woo?

LIZ   You couldn't woo our bloody cat!

                 LIZ shoves HARRY away contemptuously.

     Why, when I think of all the fine young lads from this stre
that went across to France, never again to return - bonny
strong limbed lads they were - and yet a flamin' two-in-
one like you goes out all the way to Mesopotamia, and
comes home without a scratch, I begin to lose faith in
the Almighty.

                 HARRY turns on her in a sudden quiet
                 and compelling fury.

HARRY   Shut up!   Do you hear me - shut up! - or I'll ding you
one across the chops.   Say anything you bloody want
about me, but keep my mates of Mesopotamia out of it.

LIZ   I never said anything against your mates.

HARRY   I don't care whether you did or not. I won't even have
you bringing 'em up.   That's something I try to shut
out of my mind. I wouldn't want my worst enemy to
know what we went through in that bloody country.   So
I won't stand here and listen to a woman making little of
it.

LIZ   And what about the shame we'd have suffered if I hadn't
sold my mother's things and got the money to pay the bets
eh?

HARRY (oddly eloquent and moving) Who the hell cares about
your shame or your mother's bloody trinkets. I'm talking
of things that matter. Those lads laid their lives down
without question, and now their bones lie buried in the
sand. All you women worry about is your neighbours. You
think the world starts and ends in this damn street. Well,
I were the same until I 'listed an' they sent me out to
fight in the rotten desert. And after being bloody near
marched to death, starved to death, bitten to death, and
flogged to death, I forgot all about the street. I've seen
'em die like flies from dysentery, malaria and fever. They
made us do twenty mile a day across the flamin' hot sand,
carrying full pack, parched to the guts with thirst and
blinded with the sun. You tried to keep up because if you
fell out the Turks got you. It happened to a mate of mine,
Bob Lucas, and if ever you come across a young English
lad chopped up by the Turks, it's not a sight you forget in
a hurry. Why, there's hardly a night I close my eyes that
it doesn't all come back - so I don't want you fetching it up
in my waking hours.

    LIZ goes to HARRY. He rests against
    her.

LIZ (aside) He's got round me! I might have known it...!
Useless sod he is ...! Flamin' bloody men ... they
want hanging ...

    HARRY has put his arm round LIZ, and
    we can see she hasn't a chance of holding
    out.

    Bring up sound of children singing off
    as the

    CURTAIN FALLS

ACT TWO   Scene Three

HARWOOD'S BACKYARD

> POLLY HARWOOD is whitewashing a
> wall. She works with gusto, humming
> and singing, and seemingly untroubled
> by her pregnant condition.
>
> Enter JACK carrying rolled up paper.
> He has the air of a man who doesn't
> know what it is all about.

JACK   Polly! Didn't I tell you I'd do it.

POLLY   (mimics JACK) Polly, didn't I tell you I'd do it. I can
have it done whilst you're looking at it. You can go and
varnish the chairs. (She sees paper) What's that?

JACK   Paper.

POLLY   I can see that, muggins - but what's it for?

JACK   I dunno. Mrs Sedwin gave it me - she said you'd know.

POLLY   Where's the varnish?

JACK   She wouldn't let me have it.

POLLY   What a cheek! What interference!

JACK   I didn't tell you, Polly - but you know what your mother
said -

POLLY   I don't want to know. She didn't say she'd come round,
did she! The way these women talk you'd think they
knew more about me than I know about myself.

> At that moment, on the very last word,
> POLLY feels a pain. JACK doesn't see
> her freeze. And by the time he catches
> on, it is almost over.

JACK   What's up, Polly!

POLLY   Nothing. What're you staring at?

JACK   You had a pain, didn't you?

POLLY   Don't you be such a clever Dick.

                        POLLY gets another twinge and looks
                        anxious.

JACK   I'm going off for Miss Pratt.

POLLY   You're doing nothing of the sort. You'll wait till I tell you.
                        Did you fetch that single bed down out of the back bedroom
                        like I told you?

JACK   Yes, I've put it up in front place. But why you want to be
                        downstairs when you could be upstairs where it's quiet -

POLLY   I want to see what's going on at a time like that, don't I?
                        There's no fun being stuck away in a bedroom. Besides
                        you couldn't expect Miss Pratt to go traipsing upstairs
                        every visit.

                        JACK tenderly puts arm round
                        POLLY to kiss her.

JACK   Polly love ...

POLLY   Now let's not get sloppy at a time like this.

                        She stoops from an apprehension
                        of pain.

JACK   You've got that pain again. Can I go for your mother?

POLLY   No, you can't! Oh, forgive me, Jack love, for being so
                        sharp with you.

JACK   It's all right, Polly, I understand you. Shall I - ?

POLLY   Yes do! - go on - tell her I want her - tell her -

JACK   Good.   It'll make you both happy. I'll not be a tick -
                        (Turns to go)

POLLY   No, Jack, stop! - hold on! - don't go -

                        JACK turns.

JACK   Why - what's up? - what's wrong?

POLLY   Nothing. Don't go.

JACK   Why, Polly - why not?

POLLY   I've got my pride. The pain's gone. I think I'll be able to stick it out.

                    Enter FANNY outside yard.

FANNY   (calls) Hello there! Anybody at home?

                    She touches her hair and tries to appear casual.

JACK   (amazed) It's your Mam!

POLLY   It's not, is it!

                    Tidies her appearance with alarm.

JACK   Course it is!

POLLY   I wonder what's brought her round!

JACK   To see you I expect! (Calls) Hello there! Come in, Ma! Come in ...

POLLY   (warningly) Don't you dare say anything to her about me. Remember! Not a word -

                    JACK nods. Enter FANNY with forced casual air.

FANNY   I were just passing t'backgate and I thought I'd look in -

JACK   Ee, you've arrived in the nick of ... Nice to see you.

FANNY   Nice to see you. I see you've been whitewashing -

JACK   That's right. It's dried nice, hasn't it. (Looks at POLLY appealing but gets no response)

FANNY   Yes - and it smells nice too. I always say you can't beat a bit of oldfashioned whitewash.

JACK   It beats all your newfangled stuff.

FANNY   Yes, it brightens a place. I say, doesn't it feel heavy.

JACK   Aye, there's no air about. I shouldn't be surprised if it rained.

FANNY   Neither should I.

> FANNY takes one last glimpse at
> POLLY. POLLY doesn't see it.

Ee, well - I mustn't keep you from your whitewashing,
must I?

JACK   It's all right. She's in no hurry with that.

FANNY   I suppose I'll have to be off in any case. I've got two-three
bits of washing on the line. Well, I'll go ... Ta ra for now.

> POLLY has been getting alarmed at
> the thought of FANNY going - but she
> won't give in. Then she gets a sudden
> pain. She stoops and a small cry
> escapes. JACK puts his hand out to
> her. FANNY turns back and sees her.

Polly! ...

POLLY   Mum!

> FANNY darts over to her.

FANNY   Oh, my little girl! - my Polly ...

> POLLY puts her arms round FANNY.

POLLY   Mum! Mum! Mum!

> JACK darts around in a comic fashion
> not understanding what is going on.

FANNY   Has it started, love.

POLLY   Yes, mum. Let me hold on to you.

FANNY   Hold on, love.

POLLY   Don't go away.

FANNY   I'm not going. Don't you worry.

POLLY   It hurts -

FANNY   I know. I wish I could help you.

POLLY	You are. Ee, but I'm a right softie.
FANNY	We're all softies at these times.

> JACK looks from FANNY to POLLY
> in wonder. They ignore him.

POLLY	It's gone. Oh, I have missed you, mum -
FANNY	And me you. I'm so sorry I -
POLLY	I promise you I never told a soul before you -
FANNY	I know you didn't, love.
POLLY	I've always told you everything.
FANNY	Let's not talk about it.
POLLY	I never thought how you need your mother to turn to! (She spots JACK and her manner changes) Are you still here?
JACK	Yes - why? What's wrong?
POLLY	Have you not gone for Miss Pratt yet - you great big gobbin!
JACK	You never told me to go.
POLLY	You've got to tell him everything. Ee, if they don't settle this coal strike soon, I'll go mad. I couldn't stand another eight weeks of having this chap around all the time.
·FANNY	Shall I go for her, love!
POLLY	No, let him go for what use he is. (To JACK) Go on - don't stand there skenning at me.
JACK	What shall I tell her, Polly?
POLLY	(mimic) What shall I tell her, Polly? Tell her my pains have started, you great big numskull.
JACK	All right, Polly - sorry -
POLLY	(mimic) All right, Polly! (Shouts) Get going.
JACK	I'm going.

FANNY   Call on Sarah Kippax - ask her to come round.

JACK   Righto.

Exit JACK.

POLLY   I'll feel safe with Sarah round. Oh, but he's a right mawp.

FANNY   Don't be so hard on him, love.

POLLY   I know I shouldn't be, but I can't help it. I feel he's to blame for it all. And the way he stands there staring at me with his great big gawping eyes - he seems to have come over all mard since he came out on strike. And at times I could take him in my arms and hug him.

FANNY   Why don't you?

POLLY   Ee, if I once gave way to my feelings I'd be ten times as soft as him. (Picks up brush) I'd best finish my bit of whitewashing.

FANNY   I think you can safely leave that till your next time.

POLLY   Next time! Some hopes ... (She gets pain and groans in half comic manner) ... Oooh! ...

             FANNY takes brush and leads POLLY
             into house.

             Bring up children's singing of street
             songs, off.

* * *

ACT TWO   Scene Four

HARWOOD'S LIVING ROOM

Clean, neat, occupied mainly by a
single iron bed. There is a screen
nearby. POLLY is lying in bed,
now nervous and in pain.

POLLY   (calls) Mum, how long is Miss Pratt going to be?

Enter through side door FANNY and
OLIVE carrying two kitchen chairs
and a laundry basket.

FANNY   Don't worry, love, she'll be here.

OLIVE   Unless she's got stuck somewhere on a difficult delivery,
which is always possible, yu'know. In which case we'll
have to see the job through ourselves. Eh, Fanny?

FANNY   (aside to OLIVE) Ee, I'd be no use. I feel all of a trembl
as it is.

OLIVE has put two chairs down and
rolls up her sleeves. FANNY places
the spotless laundry basket on chairs.
They drape this and turn it into an
attractive cot, and talk throughout.

OLIVE   Don't fret yourself, love. It's all a straight-forward
business, as I recall, unless of course there are compli-
cations ...

POLLY   Oh, mum, I do feel frightened.

FANNY   (hearty bluff) There's nothing to be frightened of, love.
Is there, Olive?

OLIVE   Well, I wouldn't say that ... I mean suppose it's lying the
wrong way about.

FANNY   (shuts OLIVE up) I can't understand why Sarah hasn't
arrived yet.

POLLY   It's that fool of a husband of mine. I'll bet he forgot.

OLIVE   Men are all the same when you send 'em on that sort of
errand. Mine once came back and said he couldn't find

OLIVE (Cont)	the bell on the door - and there I was in agony. Knock the bloody door in, I said to him, but get somebody. Another time - it must have been over our Meg - he came home to me and said he'd come over shy and didn't like calling on the midwife - he said something about there was a girl called Alice Entwistle as he used to go out with before he met me, standing on the step a couple of doors away and he didn't like her seeing him going for the nurse - said it made him feel a right daft thing. So I said to him, You weren't thinking of Alice flamin' Entwistle that night on the sandhills at Squire's Gate, were you ... eh? and you didn't feel such a big soft thing, did you ... eh ...?
POLLY	(groans) I know if somebody doesn't come soon - they'll be too late.
FANNY	Try not to worry, love. It'll only make you worse.
OLIVE	I was in labour for seventy-two hours over our Benny. You might be like you are now for days on end ...
POLLY	Oh, good God, I hope not! I know one thing - I'll never have another.
OLIVE	You haven't had this one yet, love. There's worse to come. They all got fed up with me, over our Benny, and at the finish I was all alone, screaming my head off when he was born. I couldn't believe I'd done it all by myself.
FANNY	(nudges OLIVE to shut up) Hush up, will you, Olive!
OLIVE	Well, you've got to say something. I find silence so depressing. Still, as my Gran used to say, if they had to have them in turn, the husband the first and the wife the second, there'd be no third!

	Enter SARAH outside. She is wearing a large
	        white starched pinafore and her appearance
	        and manner have a quiet authority in contrast
	        to what we have seen before. She carries a
	        small bag. Enters home.

SARAH	Hello there!
OLIVE	Ah, that you, Sarah?
FANNY	Ee, I'm right glad to see you.
SARAH	Where's Miss Pratt?
FANNY	She's not come yet.
SARAH	Well, don't worry, Fanny. She'll be here. She won't let us down.
OLIVE	We thought you were never coming.

SARAH	I had a bite of roast heart whilst Beatty ironed my pinafore.
OLIVE	Aye, it's not the sort of job to tackle on an empty stomach .
POLLY	Hello, Mrs Kippax.

SARAH looks down at POLLY.

SARAH	Hello, love. Got yourself in a right fix, haven't you?
POLLY	Yes - but same as I was saying, it's the last time.
SARAH	I very much doubt it.
OLIVE	We all say that over the first one, love. I remember I said it over our Win, and a year later to the day I were having our Meg. Then I said it over the twins. We women forgive too quickly - that's our trouble.
SARAH	Now let's have a look at you, lass. And try to keep one thing in mind, it's all very natural.
POLLY	Well, it doesn't feel like it.
SARAH	It will when you've had half a dozen. (Looks) Ee, you're well on the way, love. Olive, put the kettle ont' gas.
OLIVE	What for?
SARAH	We'll want some tea, won't we. This is always a thirsty job. Have you got lots of paper handy?
OLIVE	We've already put it in place. (She nods knowingly to SARAH)

OLIVE exits to kitchen.

SARAH	Fanny, have you got the bearing down towel?
FANNY	Ee, I clean forgot. I'll go and get one.

FANNY goes over to chest of drawers.

SARAH	You look all tensed up, love. Can't you relax a bit?
POLLY	I don't know where to start.
SARAH	Why don't you start with your big toe.

> FANNY brings towel which she hands
> to SARAH.

FANNY   Here you are, Sarah.

SARAH   Nay, this towel won't do, Fanny, it's too worn, it might
rip. I want a good strong bearing-down towel.

POLLY   There's a big towel there of Jack's, Mum. Never been
used since he came on strike.

FANNY   All right, love.

> Re-enter OLIVE.

OLIVE   The kettle's on, Sarah.

SARAH   Good. (Whisper) Now make a good fire in the back kitchen
grate. Understand me?

OLIVE   I've got you.

> OLIVE salutes and exits to kitchen.

> FANNY brings larger towel.

FANNY   How will this do, Sarah? (Hands her towel)

SARAH   That's more like it.

> SARAH deftly starts tying towel over
> the bedrail above POLLY's head.

(To POLLY) Have you been taking raspberry leaf tea?

POLLY   Yes, all along.

SARAH   Then your muscles should be nice and pliable. Well,
everything seems to be in good order. Now, can you
reach that?

> POLLY puts her hands up and holds
> onto towel.

POLLY   Yes, that feels all right.

SARAH   Good. Now when the time comes, love - but not before
- we'll want you to bear down on that towel. It'll help
you having something to grip to. But don't overdo it,

SARAH (Cont)	and whatever you do, don't force. Do you follow me?
POLLY	(nods) I think so.
SARAH	You're all of a sweat, lass. Let me wipe your forehead. (She wipes POLLY's forehead) It's all right, Fanny, don't worry -

During this OLIVE re-enters.

OLIVE	Aye, she's young - she can stand it. But you won't get me going through it again. You're fire's all right, Sarah.

Enter outside JACK. He knocks
and peeps in.

JACK	Hello there! It's only me.
FANNY	Hy, it's Jack.
OLIVE	What does he want.
SARAH	Well, don't let him come inside here -
OLIVE	We certainly don't want a man around - the husband least of all.

OLIVE and FANNY go to door.

Don't you come in here!

JACK	Why, what's up? - Is everything all right?
OLIVE	You should ask!
POLLY	(calls) Where's Miss Pratt? Haven't you fetched her?
JACK	She couldn't get away just yet.
OLIVE	Well, what the hell have you come for? You're no damn use.
JACK	I only want to see my wife.
POLLY	(calls) Well, I don't want to see you.
SARAH	Now don't disturb yourself, love - everything's coming along nicely. I'll be back in a minute.

SARAH makes towards back kitchen.

JACK   Let me in. Please, Fanny - just for a minute.

FANNY   (calls) Sarah - he wants to know can he come in for a minute.

SARAH   No, he can't! It was never considered lucky to have a man round at a time like this.

SARAH exits.

FANNY   She won't let you in, Jack.

JACK   Why, what have I done?

OLIVE   Listen the hard faced sod! ... what has he done! Can't you hear that poor girl moaning!

JACK   But, Fanny, I only ...

FANNY   Sorry, Jack, but we don't want any spectators on the scene. Now off with you.

OLIVE   Aye, sling your bloody hook when you're told.

OLIVE pushes protesting JACK off.

That's got rid of him -

FANNY   Do you think we were a bit too hard on the poor lad -

OLIVE   You can't be too hard on 'em in these situations. They've got to realise there's a time when men are men and women women - and no love lost between 'em.

POLLY   (cries out) Sarah! Mum! Mum!

FANNY   Coming, love.

POLLY   I want you near me. Where's Sarah?

FANNY   (calls) Sarah, hurry up!

FANNY goes to POLLY. SARAH enters carrying a small bowl and with towel over her arm, and puts them down.

SARAH	Don't worry, I'm here. You're all right, Polly, things are coming along beautifully. Just let me have another look at you.

FANNY moves away.

FANNY	Thank God you're here, Sarah.
OLIVE	I don't know what we'd have done without you. Why don't you go off, Fanny.
FANNY	No, I'll stick it out.
OLIVE	I don't know how you can stand it.

SARAH pulls back sheet.

SARAH	(surprised but calm) Ee, look at this one! - you are in a hurry, lass. You're your mother all over again ... eh, Fanny? ... You're a right quick 'un ...
FANNY	Oh, dear me ...
OLIVE	I say, Sarah, what'll we do if Miss Pratt doesn't come?
FANNY	Oh, don't say that, Olive.

POLLY lets out a frightened moan.

SARAH	(calmly) I know what we shan't do - that's get panicky.

OLIVE is losing her nerve. FANNY
is frightened but resolute.

POLLY	Sarah, Sarah!
SARAH	Yes, love. Take hold of this towel. Now what was it?

POLLY reaches up to towel.

POLLY	I feel frightened.
SARAH	I'm sure you do, lass. We all felt that way the first time. Eh, Olive?

POLLY moans.

OLIVE	(jittery) Sarah, what do you say to me dashing off and fetching Miss Pratt ...

SARAH	(looks at OLIVE) Aye, you might as well, for what use you'll be here.
OLIVE	Are you coming with me, Fanny.
FANNY	No, I'm staying here.

FANNY moves over to POLLY.

OLIVE	Toodlepip ...

OLIVE exits with undignified haste.

POLLY	Oh, mum, I'm so glad you're here.
FANNY	So'm I. How are you feeling now, love?
POLLY	Rotten.
SARAH	(amused) What a thing to say at a time like this.
POLLY	Anybody as says they don't feel rotten is a liar. I feel frightened too.
SARAH	Of course you do. You need faith, lass, and God'll give you that if you ask him.
POLLY	I've never stopped asking him ... ever since I felt that first kick ... (To FANNY) I never told anybody before you, mum ... I wouldn't ... honest ...
FANNY	(stoops over her affectionately) I know you didn't, love.

POLLY moans. FANNY moves back.

SARAH	(quietly to FANNY) She's drawing very near Fanny ... very near.
FANNY	Suppose Miss Pratt ...
SARAH	Don't worry, Fanny - I'm here ...
POLLY	Sarah ... will I be all right ...
SARAH	Course you will, love. You and your baby. I'll see you don't hurt yourself - and he'll be all right, God willing ...

POLLY whimpers.

SARAH   Easy does it, now, love ... easy ... my, you are a little
(Cont)   champion you are for sure ...

                 POLLY whimpers again and cries
                 a bit as lights fade down.

                 Cry of BABY is heard.

                 Suddenly, sharply, the bright music
                 of a barrel organ is heard.

                 Enter down front, along strip of street,
                 a MAN in old army topcoat, playing a
                 barrel organ.

                       * * *

ACT TWO   Scene Five

HARWOOD'S LIVING ROOM

The screen has been put aside. Room has
changed atmosphere, suggesting brightness
and life. MISS PRATT is packing her bag
ready to go. There are signs of tea having
been served, and happy whispering talk is
going on. LIZ and BEATTY are there, of
course, and perhaps more surprising,
HARRY and ALBERT have called in to see
newborn infant. POLLY is sitting up
drinking a cup of tea. OLIVE has more
than recovered. FANNY is quietly content.
SARAH is very modestly in authority in
the scene. The only one missing is the
father, JACK.

MISS PRATT   Well, I'd best be off - I've another call to make.

POLLY   Thank you very much!

FANNY   Yes, thank you, Miss Pratt!

MISS PRATT   No ... don't thank me - it was all over and done with when
I arrived. Thank Sarah there - she's the one - I couldn't
have done a better job myself ...

AD LIB murmurs of praise from OTHERS.
SARAH feels shy. BEATTY goes forward
and puts an arm round her.

POLLY   You'll never know what you did for me, Sarah ...

SARAH   ... Or you for me!

Nobody quite understands this but
BEATTY.

MISS PRATT   I'll call round tomorrow morning and have a look at you
and baby. Ta ra, everybody.

AD LIB's ta ra's.

... Goodbye, Sarah - and thanks.

SARAH   Goodbye, Miss Pratt.

OTHERS look to SARAH. MISS PRATT
exits.

POLLY breaks up moment by putting
down cup.

POLLY   That's the best cup of tea I ever tasted in all my
life ...

SARAH takes cup from POLLY, who lies
back in bed. WOMEN nod understandingly.

SARAH   I'll bet it was.

HARRY takes a look into the cot.

HARRY   Yu'know something, Polly, you'd have a job to say who
the baby favours. He looks like nobody I know.

WOMEN all turn on HARRY.

LIZ   Why, he's the spit image of his father.

BEATTY   Course he is. Without a doubt. You must be blind.

OTHERS ad lib "course he is" etc.

FANNY   Except he's got her father's forehead and nose.

OLIVE   Oh, yes, he's got Gilbert's nose and top of the face ...
but otherwise just like Jack.

HARRY   Yes, now you come to point it out to me, I see what you
mean.

ALBERT   He's a lovely child, God bless him, no matter who he's
like.

SARAH   Let's just say he's like himself.

OLIVE   And his dad!

POLLY   (pause) Oh, I wonder where Jack can have got to!

FANNY   Yes, it's funny he's not been back yet.

ALBERT   He were wandering about like a wet lettuce the last I
saw of him.

SARAH   I'm not surprised.

FANNY   I hope the poor lad didn't take our talking to him the
               wrong way ...

OLIVE   How could he ... !

POLLY   Sarah, do you think I should have baby in here beside me.

               Enter JACK on the strip of street outside.
               He looks anxious and uncertain.

SARAH   You could ... But I wouldn't if I were you. Take your
               ease while you can, love.

HARRY   Aye, let him get used to being on his own. He'll have a
               hard life in front of him if it's owt like mine.

POLLY   Funny, but I suddenly feel lost without Jack around.

OLIVE   I reckon you'd like to throw us all out now and just be
               here with him and the baby.

SARAH   Well, she's a mother now, so it's only natural she
               wants her man around.

               JACK knocks nervously on the door.

               Excited reaction from OTHERS.

LIZ   There's somebody there now.

BEATTY   I expect it's him

               OLIVE goes to the door and FANNY
               follows. POLLY quickly grabs a comb,
               does her hair and adjusts her nightie.

SARAH   (to POLLY) That's right - make yourself nice for him.

OLIVE   Is that you, Jack?

FANNY   (warmly) Hello, Jack love! What are you standing out
               there for ?

JACK   Why - I can't come in, can I?

               POLLY leans back on pillow and closes her
               eyes.

OLIVE	But of course you can, love! What else?
FANNY	It's your home! Come on in, lad. What's up with you.

AD LIB warm greetings.

JACK steps inside nervously,
bewildered at the change.

ALBERT	They've all been waiting for you, Jack.
SARAH	Course we have. Hello, Jack love.

JACK stands dumbfounded for a
moment and they all go quiet.

JACK	What's the news? I mean - has anything - has anything happened yet?

JACK looks round. The others leave
it to POLLY to break the news. POLLY
remains silent.

Suddenly the silence is broken by a
loud wail. JACK looks incredulous.

JACK	That's not ... it can't be - Has she had it?
FANNY	Yes, she has for sure -
SARAH	A son - seven pounds if an ounce. Not a mark on him. A beautiful child.
LIZ	You're a father, love.
JACK	Am I?
BEATTY	Congratulations, Jack.
OLIVE	Well, don't stand there.
JACK	(dazed) And what about Polly - is she all right?
HARRY	Course she bloody is - it's you as looks in need of attention, mate. Go on - don't be so backward at coming forward.
LIZ	Shut up, will you!

FANNY   Go on, Jack. She's been asking for you.

> The WOMEN watch as JACK moves towards
> the bed. He is about to look into the cot but
> changes his mind and goes slowly towards
> POLLY. The WOMEN nod understandingly
> to each other at this. He takes off his cap
> and looks down at POLLY.

JACK   Polly - Polly, love ... are you - ?

POLLY   You're back then?

JACK   Aye, I were hanging about. How are you feeling?

POLLY   I'm all right. A bit tired like.

JACK   I told you to let me do that whitewashing ...

> WOMEN react.

You look - you look different.

POLLY   Do I?

JACK   Yes, a lot. Nicer, if anything. Did it hurt you much,
Polly?

POLLY   Not all that much. Have you not seen your son yet?

JACK   My son! My - No, not yet.

> JACK turns and lifts back cover and looks
> down at child. CHILD gives a cry.
> JACK stares down without speaking, then
> looks at POLLY.

Ta, Polly. Thanks very much. I can hardly believe
he's ours.

SARAH   He's not love. They're only lent to you.

FANNY   Yes - that's what they say. Why don't you take him
up and hold him, Jack?

JACK   Me-ee, I daren't. I'm too clumsy.

POLLY   Give him to him, Mum.

OLIVE   Yes, let the proud father hold his son.

>Murmurs of agreement from others as
>FANNY picks up CHILD and hands it
>to JACK.

HARRY   Mind you don't drop it!

>LIZ and others give HARRY a look.

>JACK stares down at CHILD in silence
>for a time.

JACK   He's a bonny lad ..

FANNY   Yes - and look at all the lovely hair he's got.

HARRY   Aye - it puts me in mind of a wig.

>FANNY and others turn on HARRY.

JACK   I know one thing - I'll see he doesn't go through what I've had to go through - he'll never set foot down pit.

ALBERT   There's worse things than that.

POLLY   (to JACK) Yes - and I wouldn't have you different -

>JACK looks at POLLY somewhat
>mystified.

SARAH   She likes you as you are, Jack.

>The CHILD lets out a sudden cry.
>JACK turns to look down on him
>again and slowly a smile comes
>to his face.

JACK   (surprised) Sarah, you were right! ... yu'know - that feeling you told me about ... it's just come to me ...

>FADE UP street singing of CHILDREN
>as the

CURTAIN FALLS